I'M AWKWARD, YOU'RE AWKWARD

A BELIEVER'S GUIDE TO BEING IN THE WORLD BUT NOT OF IT

SHELBY ABBOTT

"The reason why so many people love and admire Shelby is right in this book. He's an amazing communicator, passionate about Christ, inspiring to listen to, and funnier than anyone you know. In *I'm Awkward, You're Awkward* Shelby does what Shelby always does: he uses his considerable gifts and talent to help average Christians live above average."
RICK JAMES, author *Jesus Without Religion, A Million Ways To Die*

"Shelby has a rare ability to talk about serious things in a hilarious way. He makes you laugh, and while you're holding your sides trying to catch a breath, he sneaks into your brain and makes you think."
MATT MIKALATOS, author *My Imaginary Jesus, Night of the Living Dead Christian, The Sword of Six Worlds*

"I laughed heartily and often. I love Shelby's wit. He gives great perspective on how to be relevant and relate in our culture. His personal stories and illustrations really make his points stick. In my view, no one understands how to connect with believing and non-believing college students better than Shelby. Read his book and learn from one of the best!"
ROGER HERSHEY, author *The Finishers*

"In his unique, engaging, and whimsical style, Shelby Abbott offers Christians a page-turning book that can help them understand and connect with a non-believing culture while not being less than what God calls them to be. At the heart of his stories stand the great truths and core values of biblical Christianity: God's extravagant grace, the alluring perversity of sin, the call to serious and sacrificial engagement with others, the mystery of forgiveness that is completely unearned, the offering of life in its fullness through Christ, the stench of legalistic religion, the power of the Holy Spirit to overcome our fears and awkwardness to carry out the Great Commission, and much more. Enjoyable and helpful reading!"
DR. GREGG ALLISON, author *Historical Theology: An Introduction to Christian Doctrine* and *Sojourners and Strangers: The Doctrine of the Church*
Professor of Christian Theology, The Southern Baptist Theological Seminary, Louisville, KY

Visit Shelby online at shelbyabbott.com.

I'm Awkward, You're Awkward: A Believer's Guide to Being In the World but Not Of It

Cover and interior book design by Rachael Abbott, KingFisher Media™.

Edited by Neil Downey and Byron Straughn.

All Scripture quotations, unless otherwise indicated, are taken from the Holy Bible: *New International Version.*

CONTENTS

ACKNOWLEDGMENTS

To my wife, Rachael. The blessing of being married to you is like winning the lottery every day. I strike it rich over and over again.

To my mom, Beckie, and my dad, Dave. You are great parents who have shepherded great experiences for a greatly confusing son.

To Rick James for opening doors, windows, and egresses for me.

To Neil Downey for all of your editing work, and Byron Straughn for your readjustment of my theological lenses that they might be focused appropriately.

And last but also least, to Ryan Seacrest, Tom Cruise, and Al Pacino. You make me believe that a man under 5′8″ can still aspire to tall adventures in life.

FOREWORD

By Matt Mikalatos

Shelby Abbott called me a while ago. I was really happy to hear from him, just like everyone is always really happy to hear from Shelby, because he's funny and kind and delightful. Our conversation went something like this…

Shelby: Matt, I'm writing a book called, "I'm Awkward, You're Awkward" and I was wondering if you would be willing to write the foreword?

Me: That's really flattering, Shelby, thanks. Is it because of my keen wit and intellect, or because I'm an author, or just because you respect me?

Shelby: It's because you're the most awkward person I know.

(Silence. A long, uncomfortable silence. At least once Shelby said, "Are you still there?" and I said, "Shh, I'm thinking.")

Me: Okay, I'll do it.

So, here we are. Let me start with a few things about Shelby. A lot of people know Shelby because they've seen him up front as an emcee at some big event. They think that Shelby is really cute and funny. He is. He's hilarious. I've been there to clean up afterwards. I've seen college students choke on their sodas, or pee their pants, or break their iPhones because they were laughing so hard. And he's cute, too, like Elmo or a masculine My Little Pony. Everyone wants to catch him and take him home, and put him with all their stuffed animals. Some people think that's all there is to Shelby, but they're wrong.

In fact, Shelby is one of those guys that the more you get to know him, you're forced to love him more and more forever. Even if you start out hating him (for some reason I can't fathom), all of a sudden he makes you laugh. And then he comes up and asks you how you're doing, and he really cares. He really means it. Then you meet his amazing, beautiful, talented wife. Then you see his daughter, who will teach you the true meaning of adorable. And you start to wonder, who is this guy? Then you start to talk to him and you discover that he has deep thoughts about movies, and culture, and music, and Jesus. He changes the way you look at things. He challenges you to think harder, to be more careful with your conclusions, to be serious about your faith in God. He talks a lot about how to interact with the world around us but still be serious about following Jesus.

Shelby has a rare ability to talk about serious things in a hilarious way. He makes you laugh, and while you're holding your sides trying to catch a breath, he sneaks into your brain and makes you think. He knows it's necessary to take Jesus seriously, but he also knows you can do that and still have fun. That's something that I deeply respect about Shelby.

This book is designed as something to do every day, just like sleeping, eating and brushing your teeth. Shelby's book is intended to give you a laugh and give you a thought to consider each day. It's extremely addicting to read, though, so you may find yourself sneaking in a few days at once, or flipping through the book and reading whatever catches your eye. This is to be encouraged, just like nightly sleep, snacks, and excessive brushing. And just like sleep, snacks, and too much brushing, this book is refreshing, filling, and good for you. Enjoy.

MATT MIKALATOS
Author of *My Imaginary Jesus* and *Night of the Living Dead Christian*

As long as I'm in my apartment, I'm okay.
But when I wanna go out, I get…weird.
BOB WILEY, *WHAT ABOUT BOB?*

PROLEGOMENON

(Fancy Word for Introduction)

Christians Are Awkward

At the risk of sounding dramatic, the last time I went shopping for a new backpack, I had a once in a lifetime experience. It's true... let me explain.

At this particular time in my life, I was temporarily without a car, so I had a friend of mine drive me to an outdoor shopping center in Charlottesville, Virginia, not too far from the place where I was living (that place being the second floor of my parents house). The shopping center had a variety of options for me to choose from in the hunt for the perfect new bag along with a bunch of other time-wasting shops that called to both my curiosity and spending habits.

I casually glanced out the passenger side window as we passed by the sporting goods store en route to a nearby parking space and thought about what I would look like walking into a coffee shop while carrying my things inside my precious new book-carrying apparatus. Granted, it was only in my mind, but I looked good... very good.

I smiled dreamily at the scenario, but quickly came to my senses when I spotted a guy in my line of sight that seemed remarkably familiar to me. I knew that I had never seen him before in real life and I wasn't 100% sure that it was actually him, but in that moment, I had to find out definitively if I was right about the identity of the person who had caught my attention.

"Park the car!" I yelled to my friend, "Quick, park the Car!"

"What?" she said, "What is it?"

"I think I just saw someone famous that I have to meet, so park the car in the next spot you find!"

She did so, and before the vehicle even came to a complete stop, I jumped out and started sprinting across the parking lot in the direction that I thought the famous person was headed.

I remember hearing my friend yell at me from behind, "What are you going to do when you get there?" Good question. I thought about that for a second as I ran and eventually shouted back, "I don't know!" Other than that, the only thing I heard in my dash to see this man was the sound of the wind in my ears as I raced down the sidewalk. I distinctly remembered that he was wearing a red shirt, so that's what I looked for when I passed each storefront, one after the other.

I stopped dead in my tracks when I spotted a blurry image of a man in a red shirt hovered behind a counter inside the glass doors. I quickly entered and got a better look at the man I was chasing as he purchased his items and subsequently signed an autograph for the worker behind the counter. Yep, it was him, alright. I had successfully tracked down the one and only Dave Matthews (He's got a band named after him).

I shot to the back of the store and nuzzled up next to him at the counter. He immediately sensed that someone was much too close to his personal space and looked over at me, quizzically. I quickly ripped a piece of paper off of a sweepstakes entry pad on the counter, flipped it over and said, "Hi Dave. Can you sign an autograph for me too?"

He smiled a bit and graciously said, "Sure. What's your name?"

"Shelby," I said and nervously handed him the paper.

I couldn't believe that I was actually standing there next to one of my favorite musical artists of all time. It was overwhelming. My mouth went dry and my armpits went wet. I felt a little shaky, but my mind knew that this was it. This was my moment. My one moment in time where I stood face to face with Dave Matthews and could say practically anything in order to leave an indelible impact so that I could be remembered by him for all time. *Think of something good, you idiot,* I thought to myself...and as he handed the autograph back to me, I opened my mouth only to have this come out:

"Hey Dave. Can I call you Dave? Anyway...uh, you performed

a concert at my campus last semester and I heard it was great. I was gonna go and everything, but the tickets were $75 and I just didn't want to pay that much."

That was it. That is what I chose to say to Dave Matthews in my one moment. Talk about blowing it.

He was nice, though, and muttered something about how a lot of things are too expensive now. We both walked to the front of the store together, I opened the door for him (because I'm a gentleman), and we then went our own separate ways.

As I walked back to find my friend that I ditched in the parking lot, there was only one pervasive thought that rolled around in my mind: *Man, Shelby, you are awkward.*

It's true. I am awkward.

I'm not exactly sure when I became that way, but I think it might have been right around the time that I became a Christian. My guess is that someone from an underground corporation run by TBN and the guys that wrote the *Left Behind* series snuck into my dorm room the night after I made a public profession of Christian belief, and injected some sort of serum in my neck that made me super weird. I can't really prove it, but that's the theory I'm currently running with.

In the years following my conversion, I've spent a significant amount of time with other Christians and am now even a full time missionary, working with college students (both Christian and not Christian) on a daily basis. My interactions with these other followers of Christ have reinforced my belief that perhaps I wasn't the only one to be injected with the syringe of awkward serum.

Why is that? I find it strange that the people who darken the doorway of America's churches each Sunday (for the most part) have a consistent awkward quality about them. Seriously, I can't count how many times I've had a conversation with another Christian and then walked away saying to myself, "Hmm. Well, that was weird."

I'm not necessarily saying that this is a bad thing, though. Not at all. Regardless of whether or not they are a Christian, awkward people make the world a better place to live. What would the fabric of society look like without the Dwight Schrutes and Conan O'Briens? The Ben Steins or the Tina Feys? The answer is "boring."

No, I'm not ragging on all of the "awkwards" out there; I'm celebrating them! Heck, I am one and I embrace it with joy. What I am saying, however, is that there seems to be a looming personality likeness within the subculture of American Christianity that has become the prevalent personality type. In short: most Christians are awkward.

And since I believe that to be true, I think my belief carries with it a potential obstacle on the journey of life lived within the calling of every Jesus follower—how do we connect with the non-believing culture at large while not compromising who God has biblically called us to be? Can there really be a balance between the two extremes? Is it truly possible to be in the world but not of the world?

Welcome to my own personal wrestling match. This book will attempt to address those questions while candidly pointing to the fact that the process is difficult and mostly bizarre. I can't say that I'm the guy with the answers to your burning awkward questions and pursuits, but I'd be more than happy to be your tour guide on this funky voyage we call "Being an Awkward Christian."

Takin' It to the Next Level

The story is told of three military recruiters being invited to a high school assembly for the purpose of communicating the benefits of military life after graduation. The assembly gathered in the gymnasium and all the students took their seats on the wooden bleachers. The principal of the school was emphatic that each of the recruiters only speak to the assembly for 20 minutes so that they would all have equal time before the hour-long meeting was over, after which the students would be able to check out their booths if they wanted more specific information on how to join a certain branch.

The recruiter for the Army was up first and he spoke passionately about how great the Army was and why each and every student there should join. His zeal led him to talk for 25 minutes.

Not to be outdone, the Navy representative got up and spoke with great fervor about why the students in attendance should consider joining the Navy. His enthusiasm led to a verbose 30 minutes.

Up last was the recruiter for the Marines, and all that remained of the hour was a measly 5 minutes. The officer stood to his feet and paced in front of the crowd. Nearly 4 minutes passed as he moved back and forth like a caged lion in tense quietness.

When he finally broke the silence, he said, "In a crowd this size, I doubt that maybe 1 or 2 of you are good enough to call yourself a Marine. If those 1 or 2 could come see me at my booth afterward, I would appreciate it. Thank you." Then he sat down.

After the assembly was over, guess whose line was the longest at their booth? Yep, you guessed it—the Marine's.

See, the truth is that a person responds when the bar is raised in their life...they really do. And that's essentially what this book is about: raising the bar in your life.

My hope is that you respond to the things I have to say with excitement, vigor, and passion as you consider what God might have in store for you in your natural circle of influence. But first we must discuss a few things...

I Really Have No Clue What to Say Right Now

Connecting with people is pretty hard to do even when we are comfortable with the topic of conversation. It's been said that everyone communicates, but few connect. The idea for Christians communicating with non-Christians is, of course, to connect. And if, all of a sudden, you decide to throw spiritual things into the mix on top of the already difficult task of enhancing natural human relations with people, an eerie sense of awkwardness creeps into the conversation and your worst fears have come to fruition: you've been labeled a "religious nut."

Well, worry not, my spiritual freak shows. I hope to ease that awkward tension you might be feeling in those interactions with people by giving you a guide. A guide that works by providing stories, illustrations, anecdotes, and lessons in small, digestable bites for the purpose of motivation.

Why small sections, you ask? Because the average person today has the attention span of a squirrel on Red Bull, so I'm going to assume that you are that type of person and not someone who enjoys reading *War and Peace* in your free time on the weekends. The easier to plow through, the better, right? Ask any construction worker on a backhoe and he'll tell you. (That was a joke.)

This book is meant to help maneuver you through the thick and bizarre waters of communication with people that don't believe the same thing that you do (I'm making the assumption that you are a follower of Jesus Christ). It's meant to help you understand that it really is possible to be *in* the world but not *of* the world and unapologetically represent your faith.

Is it okay to be funny and make fun of yourself as a quirky Christian? How do you find the middle ground between legalism and license while not feeling like a fundamentalist or spiritual loser? Is it permissible to poke fun at other people for the silly things they do/say and not offend those that aren't Christians?

These are the types of questions that I hope to answer (and more) because I truly feel that if you are keeping in step with what God has for your life, you will have an authentic desire to tell others about the only relationship in your life that is 100% fulfilling—your relationship with God through Jesus Christ.

As we read through the pages of the New Testament, one thing begins to become abundantly clear: there is a reality that Jesus' instruction to tell everyone about Him wasn't just for the twelve disciples…it was for all people who claim to be His followers, including us today. He plainly commands each of us to represent Him where we are and where we will be, regardless of age, occupation, sex or race. If you are a follower of Christ and find yourself frustrated by your lack of motivation or ability to accurately communicate your faith to others, then this just might be the resource you've been looking for. (If you're not motivated and simply don't care about talking to others about God, please put this book down now and go watch TV or something.)

I've found that with many Christians, the desire to make connections with their non-believing friends is so great that the dam is almost bursting with the impulse to reach out. They simply lack the tools to initiate appropriately. If I can help by nudging you in the right direction, maybe we will begin to see a lot more accurate representations of Christ out there, engaging in the lives of those who don't believe, while living as legitimate examples of Jesus followers.

We shall see, oh yes, we shall see.

Choose Your Own Adventure

Remember those old books that let you choose what would happen next in the story based upon what you wanted the character to do? They'd say something like,

"If you want Gary to climb up the rock wall and into the cave to explore what danger lurks inside, turn to page 61."

or

"If you want Gary to return back to town and call the police because he has just witnessed a beheading, turn to page 84."

Those books created a new wrinkle in the reading experience for kids that made picking up a book a little less mundane and a lot more exciting. Now, this book isn't quite at the interaction level of a "Choose Your Own Adventure" novel, but it isn't necessarily a book you have to read in a linear fashion either.

When you pick up a guide on virtually anything, you explore its contents in nearly the same way that you would a tell-all handbook about your favorite theme park or musical artist. It's meant to be thumbed through, explored sporadically, examined out of order, and referenced when a specific question pops into your mind about a certain subject. Such is the spirit in which I've created this guide.

If you want information on one topic this book addresses, don't feel like you have to read all of the preceding sections in order to understand what is communicated later in the writing. Yes, as a whole, the picture I'm painting makes more sense if you have ingested the entire package, but as far as I'm concerned, if I can help you by informing and instructing in any area at any time, it's all good.

Okay. Now that we've got the preliminary stuff out of the way, let's get rolling on the practical things that will lead us through the murky waters of being a Christ-follower in this crazy world.[1]

For your ease of use, I've broken it all down into four sections that will serve as guideposts or departments, depending on where you find yourself in any given social situation. They are: *Things About the World, Things That Get in Your Way, Things to Motivate You, and Things That Help You Get Things Done.*

Pretty straight forward, I know, but I simply tried to think about what I would want to know, depending on what I was going through at the time. I hope they are helpful to you and beneficial to your personal awkward journey.

Have fun.

PART ONE

THINGS ABOUT THE WORLD

INTRODUCTION: LAND OF THE LOST

There's a legitimate reason why TMZ is in business and doing quite well.

There is a reason why foul-mouthed and moderately talented comedians rise to the levels of fame that they do.

There's a justifiable basis for the fact that hundreds of millions of dollars can be spent to make a movie that's labeled "so-so" during the largest economic recession since the great depression.

There truly is an explanation for the fact that Americans squabble for the scraps from Apple, Inc.'s table. (Imagine that last sentence with a Scottish accent.)

What's the reason? It is simply this: the world is a profoundly screwed up place.

As we dive in here, I think it's important that you are aware of the world's screwed-upness (in case you didn't know) before we decide to move on to more particular matters. Yes, it might seem obvious to you that there are bad things that happen around the world on a continuous basis, but sometimes it takes pointing out a few relatable specifics to someone before they will actually get the point.

For example, are you surprised that pretty much all the news that comes on your TV in the evening or over the web is bad news? Are you really all that shocked to hear that another celebrity couple has filed for divorce? Are you really that bewildered by the fact that some people have completely devoted their entire lives to the obsession of collecting *Star Wars* memorabilia? Is it appalling to you that the more wretched and edgy something is in the media, the more press it gets? Why?

My point here is that Christians are continually horrified by the lostness of this world and honestly, we really shouldn't be. Of course people are constantly sleeping around with multiple sexual partners. Of course people think that alcohol will make their problems go away. Of course profanity and filth is exalted at the highest platforms of Hollywood in the name of innovation and creativity. People are lost and they don't know any better, so why do you expect them to just behave and be good?

When quoting from the Psalms, Paul says in Romans 3:10-11:

None is righteous, no, not one; no one understands; no one seeks for God.

I hate to break it to you, but what was true back then in biblical times is true right now. For thousands and thousands of years, people have chosen noncreative ways to get into noncreative trouble.

I know a lot of Christians that think today's non-believer is far more wretched than the non-believer of yesteryear. But the truth is that sin is just carbon copied from generation to generation. We're all doing the same stupid garbage that everyone else has done since the onset of evil in Genesis 3.

Frankly, the only time I'm really surprised is when someone goes out of their way to be extraordinarily nice. That is what seems out of character for the run-of-the-mill non-Christian.

It is in the nature of every man and woman to be self-centered and tarnished, so if you are a Christian that expects every person you come in contact with to be morally exceptional, you have completely unrealistic expectations of the world. We must be aware of what is going on with our environment and whom we are trying to relate with. If we fail to take this essential first step of educating ourselves, we fail completely.

The guide begins by becoming familiar with the journey that is about to take place, and that means studying the territory into which we step. If we are blind, deaf, and dumb going in, our impact, relevance, and influence will be minimal. School starts here.

1
BACK TO THE FUTURE

Disappointment comes from unmet expectations.
ROGER HERSHEY

I'd be lying if I said that I didn't have high hopes for the future. In my mind, this present (the future according to myself back in 1989) is already somewhat of a disappointment simply because we are nowhere near the kind of technology portrayed so vividly in the movie *Back to the Future: Part 2*.

Although the plot of *Back to the Future: Part 2* was essentially just a ruse to get moviegoers to shell out more money to go and see *Back to the Future: Part 3*, I loved the 20 to 25 minute segment of that film that gave us a Spielberg-imagined window into the potential time to come. I remember thinking how cool it would be to live in a time where garbage could be turned into fuel and dogs could be walked by robotic powered leashes. That movie opened up my imagination in ways that no other flick had, and it was easy to imagine myself as the lead character[2] in that future, tumbling around town with awestruck wonder because everything around me was just so incredibly amazing.

But now here I sit, caught up in the timeline with that grand vision of the future, yet there is no hover-board floating in my closet. I don't have a pair of Nike high top shoes with power laces. If I ever inadvertently fell into a man-made lagoon lake in front of a clock tower and got completely drenched in the process, my jacket would not blow dry itself and state to me in a robot voice, "Your jacket is now dry." What a letdown.

Things just don't seem to fly as much in the real future as compared to the movie version of it. You know what I mean? Cars, bikes, skate boards, trashcans, you name it—everything in the future is able to fly when you see it in the movies. Where the heck is my flying car? My floating robot butler? My hovering cupcake dispenser? With the obvious exception of the iPhone, my hopeful vision of the future has been dashed by the continual ground-dwelling apathy in which we humans exist (I know the iPhone can't float, but I'm sure it will be able to in a very near firmware update).

My point is, if you expect something to be true and reality proves itself to be contrary to that expectation, disappointment is an unavoidable reaction. In short, disappointment comes from unmet expectations.

I am no stranger to this feeling. My life has continually been peppered with disappointment in everything from how long I had to wait in line for that awesome roller coaster at Busch Gardens Williamsburg back in 8th grade, to finding out that my natural father was someone who said that he loved me, but in his actions really never showed me any kind of love at all.

I would imagine that if you thought hard about it, you could probably come up with a long list of all your disappointments in life too. Anyone could. However, I'm not going to ask you to do that right now (save that exercise for your psychiatrist). What I will ask you to do is to set yourself up for satisfaction by having the proper perspective on what the world is and what it is not.

We are living in a time that is ever-increasingly disenchanted by a person who communicates their faith in a way that implies that they are correct and everyone else is incorrect. Essentially, sharing the gospel has gradually become a secular sin. In a talk I once heard him give, Tim Keller put it this way:

> *Sixty years ago in our culture, evangelism was an irritation. Today, it's offensive...it's an offense. Today, believe it or not, evangelism is one of the few secular sins. People will say, "If you (as a Christian) tell me that I must believe what you believe, that's wrong, it's narrow-minded, it's offensive...it's bad for our culture!"*

In the old days, you used to have to do apologetics for the gospel. Now, you have to do apologetics for apologetics.[3]

What once was a small hurdle to be jumped over is now a very large wall to be climbed. Do not deceive yourself; our spiritual climate has changed. On the whole, people won't give you the benefit of the doubt that there is a universal and absolute truth. They won't assume that there has got to be one correct way to make yourself right with God. Honestly, they probably won't even assume that there is a God capable of being known.

Talking to people about God is a lot more difficult than it used to be because we are essentially one step further away from being able to share the message of salvation. As Keller puts it, "Now, you have to do apologetics for apologetics."

The reason I bring this up is because I believe that many well-intended churchgoers in America think that the present-day culture is the same as it used to be back in the late 90s or early 2000s and they believe it's easy to share the gospel in the same way that it's "always been done." Or even worse (not necessarily 'worse' but more incorrect assumptions), a lot of Christians incorrectly assume that if they simply invite their friends to a Sunday morning service where there is an open invitation to accept Christ, they've actually shared the gospel with said friend.

I hate to break it to you, but that approach to communicating the gospel is a lazy one in this day and age. It is going to take a lot more effort on the part of every Christ-follower out there to reach those who need to hear and receive the redemption message that can change their lives.

With very few exceptions, you can't just fire off a quick gospel presentation and ask for a response anymore. That's awkward. You can't just invite someone to church and give him or her a nudge to raise their hand when an invitation is given. That's even more awkward. It's a different world now than it used to be and I'm positive that you will be sorely disappointed if you expect it to be otherwise.

People want to be brought into a story. They want to be listened to and cared for. People want authenticity and genuine concern... and if you fake it, they'll know. Doing apologetics for apologetics requires exploration of people on their terms, not yours. It necessitates research, time, care, love, prayer, and Spirit-led discernment (at the risk of infringing on your schedule or agenda).

Am I making sense here? I hope so, because if this seems rather obvious to you, you're in a much better place than a vast percentage of Christians today. However, if what I'm presenting is new information, that's okay too!

It's been said that education without action is progression to destruction. Well, maybe nobody ever said anything like that before, but I really do think I'm giving you pearls here, my friends. The next step is yours for the taking.

Am I disappointed by the obvious absence of the wonderful things presented in the possible timeline of *Back to the Future: Part 2*? Yes, of course. But deep down, I know my expectations are in the wrong place for assuming such an existence. If I know the truth about the environment in which I live and eliminate the tempting desire to do "ministry as usual" I won't be shocked by what I find when I do share my faith and I won't be disappointed because my proper expectations have nipped that disappointment in the bud.

It's a win/win, really.

2
BEING A FEMALE FRESHMAN

Through a series of events a few years ago, I ran across a poem that was written and published in a mid-western college campus newspaper that struck me. I was surprised when I read it because the author was very honest about...well, everything she seemed to be going through at the time she penned it.

Written by a freshman woman and printed anonymously in her school paper, the poem is a very raw representation of what a lot of college females go through the first year they are away from home at school. More than that, though, I believe this is an interesting window into the hearts of everyone who longs to be loved, and who will claw for that love in any way they can.

Let me warn you before you read on: this poem is an honest look into the life of this girl and I haven't edited it for the sake of appropriateness. They are her words and I felt it was best to include all of them as she wrote them. It is in no way G-rated.

Now, after that disclaimer, feel free to read on if you wish. The poem is entitled *I Am a Female Freshman.*

I am a female freshman.
I live in a 2 ft. by 2 ft. prison cell.
My roommate has sex when I am in the room.
I've gained 15 pounds or more since August.
I got more ass in the first 2 weeks of college than ever before.
I now get less ass than ever before.
I drink Beast from a keg and Nattie Light from a can.
I pretend to believe frat guys even though I know they suck...
I just want some ass.
I wear a pea coat, tight black bootie pants, tank tops, and platforms.

I have a 2.1 GPA.
I walk in the dark, cold rain for a beer, but I won't walk to classes in the same weather.
I never make my 8:00 class.

I am a female freshman.

I have been molested on the dance floor.
I have hooked up with all the guys in my dorm.
I have mono.
I don't sleep, except through classes.
I survive on power naps.

I am a female freshman.

I drink more vodka than water.
My new best friend is the toilet.
I black out for extended lengths of time.

I am a female freshman.

I've learned what it means to re-wear clothes until they are so dirty they are stiff.
I'm familiar with the vague embarrassed feeling the morning after a night of complete unadulterated drunkenness.

I am a female freshman.

I promised myself that I will work off that large pizza I ate last night…
Tomorrow, maybe…

I've learned, to my dismay, that college boys are the same as high school boys...a year or two older.

I am a female freshman.

Again, this is a real look into the soul of a woman that's pretty truthful about her experiences. Yet in a way, she seems very fed up with life as it sits for her. She seems sad, doesn't she? Hopeless... but still searching.

I like to read this poem to certain groups of people that need to be awakened to the actual nature of the world just beyond their ministry or church doors. Many times, Christians are unaware of what other people go through on a day-to-day basis and can forget that there are real human beings out there searching for genuine fulfillment in a lot of dangerous places. Those searchers need to be given the option of selecting real fulfillment, and God chooses to use His children (us) to present them with that option.

Of course, the interesting thing here is that all of us are (in a way) the female freshman from this poem. At one point and time in our lives, we were (or perhaps still are) looking for happiness and satisfaction in all the wrong places. Our hearts are hard-wired for relationship and the only way that this longing can be fulfilled is if we are reconnected with the Maker of our souls. No other substitute will be enough.

People need to be shown this. They need to see that the thing they are actually searching for in booze, sex, food, money, boyfriends/ girlfriends, technology, etc., is actually something that can only be found in God alone through Jesus Christ. He is the answer. The only answer. Not Him plus something else. Not religion or religious activity. Not behavior modification. Jesus and Jesus alone.

If we step into the world of the 'female freshman' and tell her what the answer is by not only speaking it, but also living it, she will see the contrast between genuine love and the sugar substitute that the world offers in bulk. The choice is then hers to make.

Probably the next logical question we need to ask ourselves, though, is, "Do I really believe this myself?" Well, do you?

I'll admit that it's hard for me to consistently live like Jesus is the only true avenue to satisfaction when there are so many other shiny things that scream for my attention. For example, it's really easy for me to think that the next great Apple product is going to be the answer to all my problems and make me feel better about myself. I swallow that pill every time there's a new Apple release. And if I do end up buying it, I feel disappointed that it didn't satisfy the exact way that I wanted it to.

Inevitably, I end up doing the proverbial head slap and say to myself, "It's not Christ plus something else, Shelby! How many times is it going to take for you to learn this?" Unfortunately, probably one more.

I'm fickle that way. I think we all are. Adding on to a relationship with Christ for fulfillment is something nearly all American Christians wrestle with because our hearts are capricious.[4]

The good news, however, is that Jesus will *always* be there waiting for us to return to Him for true life and fulfillment. And as we live out returning to Him time after time, others will see the weight of a real loving relationship and long for the same.

Return to Him once again *in front of* someone else. Tell them how stupid you were to believe that anything else besides Christ could satisfy you. Love on Him publically and let Him love on you. It'll just be a matter of time before the public's heart will turn soft to His calling for them too.

3
BURGER KING SPIRITUALITY

I don't need to define myself to any community by putting myself in a box labeled Baptist, or Catholic, or Muslim. When I die, I believe all my accounting will be done to God, and that when I enter the eternal realm, I will not walk though a door with a label on it.

HEATHER CARIOU, A NEW YORK CITY-BASED AUTHOR

If you really want to know what someone is passionate about or what is at the core of their belief system, just check out their bumper stickers. Seriously, this is how Americans choose to express themselves as of late. Political views, sports team affiliations, religious preferences, or how they spend their down time—it's all right there, plastered to the back of their vehicle.

In addition to their passions, you can probably make a pretty good guess at what their occupation may be as well by doing a little bumper sticker reading. For example, if they have a decal that says, "Xavier's School for Gifted Youngsters Dropout," they probably work at a comic book store. Or if their sticker exclaims, "Heck is for people who don't believe in Gosh," they most likely work at a Christian bookstore.

See what I mean?

Interestingly enough, the people that choose to express their religious views on their cars are often the people with the least amount of tolerance for open discussion about the reality of universal truth. I've heard it time and time again from both college students and professors: "That's great for you, but I believe what I believe."

My inevitable next question is usually, "Where did you come up with your beliefs?"

The response I get most often is, "It's basically a collection of beliefs I have picked up in my life over time."

This postmodern response is what is commonly referred to as "Burger King Spirituality." The reason it's called that is because Burger King's slogan is "Have It Your Way." While this may be good for the burger industry, it is phenomenally destructive as a spiritual life course. My philosophy is this: When you're dealing with eternity, it's best not to treat the experience like a spiritual buffet line. If you're operating in the realm of issues that deal with the destiny of your soul, the cavalier attitude of, "Oh, I'll have a little bit of this, and a little bit of that, and a smidge of this doctrine, and a sprinkle of that teaching," can have perpetually unfavorable repercussions.

But alas, this is the reality of our environment. Everybody is picking and choosing what they want to believe and the concept of "religion" is a bitter taste in the mouths of those that are seeking.

June-Ann Greeley, a theology and philosophy professor at Sacred Heart University in Connecticut, said this in an interview with CNN.com:

> *People seem not to have the time nor the energy or interest to delve deeply into any one faith or religious tradition. Being a spiritual Lone Ranger fits the tenor of our times. Religion demands that we accord to human existence some absolutes and eternal truths, and in a post-modern culture, that becomes all but impossible.*[5]

Is there an undertone of laziness in this quote? Yes, but I believe when someone comes face-to-face with the possibility of a relationship with the Almighty God, they'll be quick to turn off the TV, get off their butt, and pursue Him with vigor. However, as we examine what Greeley is saying, lethargy is not the real problem here. No, the actual problem is the lack of conviction for absolute and eternal truth.

At this point, I could delve into a list of apologetics for the existence of absolute truth, but that's already been done to near perfection in books like C.S. Lewis' *Mere Christianity*, and Tim Keller's *The Reason for God*. That being said, anything I could come up with would pale in comparison to those works of brilliance.

Instead, I would advise you to fight this dispersion of belief in no absolute truth by actively displaying the truth with your life. What does that mean? Simply this: the best apologetic for a life that has been changed by the Living God through Jesus Christ is a life lived differently in contrast to the norm.

If you are intentional about living the Christian life in front of those in your natural circles of influence, something will eventually stick out as different about you, inevitably raising some serious questions in the lives of those who choose relativity over truth. See, relativity, as hip as it may be right now, is shaky and unstable ground on which to build your life, and people will be inexplicably drawn to the firm concrete foundation of the Christ-centered life if you are unafraid to publicly display it. It may feel awkward in those real-life moments when you live it out, but I promise it will be attractive to onlookers who are living a hollow life without God.

Let me be clear: I'm not talking about pushing your beliefs on everyone in every conversation you have. I'm talking about not hiding the fact that you pray, you are a person of faith, you read your bible and believe what it says, you are kind and giving, you listen and are generous, you love Jesus and make Him the center of your home. In short—you are an unapologetic follower of Jesus Christ because He is the only source of abundant life.

This process will take some time, but eventually it will sharply contrast with a wishy-washy faith that is built on a hodge-podge collection of random beliefs.

Living an upfront life that follows Christ is a remarkable reality that shakes the "have it your way" spiritual mentality of our society. Besides, if truth can be that easily dissected and then reconstructed to someone's individual specifications, it's nothing that I would really choose to base my life on anyway. Would you?

Consequently, here's my new slogan for relativism: Good for burgers, bad for eternity.

4
TELEVISION DRAMA AND PERCOCET DON'T MIX

A few years ago I had my tonsils taken out. Now, this is a pretty common minor surgery, but it is surgery nonetheless. The doctors use anesthetic, they cut out some lymphoepithelial tissue, and you wake up in the recovery room with an extremely soar throat. And contrary to popular belief, no ice cream is allowed until 24 to 48 hours after the surgery is performed. Bummer, huh?

Although this procedure is fairly common amongst children because they are often prone to continued bouts of sickness, I endured the procedure when I was in my late 20's. They say that the younger you are, the easier it is to recover from this particular surgery, and it is my firm belief that "they" are very much correct. I had a pretty rough time during the week that followed my time under the knife, and the post-op pain left me boarded up in my bedroom with nothing but *24: Season 3* and a bottle of narcotic pain-killers called Percocet.

Before you jump to any conclusions, I need you to know that I don't have one of those life stories that includes a past full of substance abuse, so these kinds of drugs were a new thing to me. I was completely unaware of the potential side effects they would shepherd into my little life. Hallucinations, to be specific.

After the first day of being miserable every time I swallowed, I decided that I wanted to get some truly uninterrupted sleep that night, so just before I killed the lights, I took two Percocet pills and shut my eyes. Now, prior to my first night's sleep that evening, I had literally spent the entire day watching episode after episode of *24*, which is, of course, the beauty of television on DVD—no commercials. What I didn't realize, however, was that once you ingest that much thrilling and dramatic TV, your brain absorbs it in such a way that you can no longer think about anything else in the world. Now add a couple of narcotic pills to the mix, and you've got a pretty good recipe for a surreal mind trip.

About two hours after I fell asleep, I jolted awake to a shadowy male figure standing at the side of my bed with his arms extended toward me and his hands wrapped around my throat. To put it mildly, I freaked out.

While I struggled violently and kicked the sheets off me, I simultaneously reached for my neck, and tried to pull his hands away. Only then did I realize that there were no hands to be pulled away from the attempted murder that I was imagining. A couple of minutes went by and it finally registered with me that a cocktail of about eight episodes of *24* plus two narcotic pain-killers forms a pretty dramatic visualization of someone trying to kill you.

I vowed that night to never again take those pain meds before I went to sleep if the media I consumed that day had anything to do with terrorism, firearms, or torture. I'm happy to say that I've been hallucination-free ever since.

Whenever I think back on my little manic episode, I can't help but blame the outside influences that altered my perception of reality. It took only a couple of factors to completely convince me that my life was in danger and I was probably going to be choked out by a sinister terrorist who had somehow made his way into my suburban apartment. Sure, it sounds silly now, but it was thoroughly convincing then.

Likewise, any outside influences that meddle in our understanding of the truth deserve to be targeted and subsequently acknowledged as dangerous before we can genuinely be an effective believer that is in the world but not of it. There are countless examples of what those influences might be, and they are most likely different for each person. The key is to figure out which of those influences resonates most with your sinful tendencies to distract and lure you away into spiritual blindness. Only then will you have the wherewithal to remain immune to the relentless coaxing of the world.

I have seen numerous people in my life who have fallen prey to the wooing of the world. Being in ministry with college students gives you a front row seat to the drama of multiple lives and sometimes those dramas turn out to be tragedies. Something comes along to hypnotize a young man or woman into believing that God really isn't all that great and maybe something else would be much more fulfilling to their soul.

From what I perceive, a lot of times that "something" is sex or money. I suppose those specific "somethings" are probably no different outside of the college atmosphere. Nonetheless, I'm sure there are plenty of other "somethings" that act as siren calls to American believers, convincing them that sinful things aren't that big of a deal or that being a Christian is vapid.[6]

Lies like these are garden-variety weapons in the world's arsenal that attempt to extinguish any kind of exceptional passion you have for Jesus Christ and His desire to reach the world. Don't ignore them or think that they will just go away over time, because they won't. The world and its values are incredibly resilient in their methods of diversion.

Much like the combination of dramatic television and Percocet, many things will distort your view of reality and this is why it is so important to filter your perceptions of life through the purity of Scripture. When we are bible-dwelling followers of Jesus, the influences that try to sidetrack us (as the old hymn says) "grow strangely dim in the light of His glory and grace." In an insane world, the bible is the voice of sanity that leads every Christian who listens and believes it into a proper understanding of at least two things: the setting in which they live and the role that God has chosen for them within it by His sovereign guidance.

Oswald Chambers once said,

> *Spend plenty of time with God. Let other things go. Don't neglect him.*[7]

This is a brilliant admonition from a godly man. To say that he was on to something is a huge understatement. Reality is found in the pages of Scripture and those who connect with it regularly are able to distinguish truth from lies. Simply put, the Bible is the primary means by which a believer connects with God.

A choice must be made by each of us to determine who and what our influences will be. Those influences will come from something solid (like the bible) or something fabricated.

Choose wisely.

5
I'LL TAKE A GINGER ALE

A buddy of mine used to be a waiter at a chain restaurant back when he was in college. Needless to say, he has quite a few entertaining stories about his various experiences with rude and crazy customers. Some people are just weird.

But in addition to that, he can recount with ease some of the "behind-the-scenes" exploits of the wait/cooking staff that would probably make you shiver with disgust at what exactly goes on with food prep when no one is looking. I won't get into any of the specifics that will make you think twice about taking a loved one out to dinner on a Friday night, but I will mention one thing he told me that caught my attention and kind of made me smile.

It seems that when it came to the specific restaurant that my friend worked at, getting a ginger ale for a customer was a bit of an annoyance if they asked for one. At the standard drink dispenser that the waiters and waitresses would use to fill and refill beverage orders, the ginger ale fountain didn't exist. Ginger ale could only be dispensed from the bar. So if anyone wanted a ginger ale, the wait staff would have to walk to the other side of the restaurant where the bar was and bother the bartender, who was constantly busy in his own little drink-ordering world. To say the least, it was aggravating for all the workers involved when it came to serving a ginger ale.

After a few weeks on the job, my friend got savvy and decided to perform a little experiment that would save him both time and irritation if he could pull it off. He made a bet with a fellow coworker that he could trick the customer that ordered a ginger ale into believing that what they were drinking was their desired beverage simply by filling their glass with 97% Sprite and a quick splash of

Diet Coke. The concoction would look roughly the same as a ginger ale, plus the sweetness of it would be a sufficient substitute for the other sought-after soda. If the customer would drink it and notice a drastic difference, he would simply apologize and go to the bar for the real thing…but if they didn't notice, he would save himself tons of time and a lot of unnecessary trips to the disgruntled bartender behind the counter.

So what happened?

Well, the gamble paid off. My friend told me that in the months and months that he worked there, not one person could tell the difference between a normal ginger ale and the Sprite/Diet Coke mix. I suspect it's because people just expected that what they were drinking was something that they had ordered, so their mind led them to believe that they were consuming ginger ale and nothing else, even if it tasted different from what they would ordinarily expect from a ginger ale.

For some reason, I found this story to be completely fascinating when my friend told it to me. At first, it was hard to believe that people wouldn't be able to tell the difference between the real thing and the fake. But as I gave it some more thought, I began to understand why any unassuming restaurant patron would be duped by the faux ginger ale.

There really is no reason for us to be distrusting of our waiter or waitress when we go out to a restaurant, is there? They're generally friendly and probably want a good tip, so why would they do anything that was purposefully deceiving when it came to what kind of food or drink I ordered? I have no doubts about their desire to serve and please me the best way they know how, so my blind belief in their integrity is warranted.

But from the story I've just shared with you, maybe it isn't.

When it comes to believing the best in what the world will offer to you, we've all been duped. The popular belief that churning yourself through the "American Dream Machine" will produce joy and satisfaction is a lie.

We long for the outcomes that the world advertises through the popular avenues of wealth, possessions, prominence, recognition, and fame. But expecting these roads to lead us to actual joy and genuine satisfaction is foolish. What we've ordered is not the same as what we've received, yet because it looks the same as the real thing and we trust the deliverer, we gulp it down without hesitation.

I can come up with one too many examples of people who have searched for joy and satisfaction through the things of this world, expecting to see those desires come to fruition, yet have wound up with devastating disappointment because the world's promise of fulfillment ultimately proved hollow.

Women choosing the avenue of sex to receive love from a man. Men acquiring money in order to gain respect from their peers. High school students chasing the perfect academic record so that they'll get accepted by the right school that will ultimately lead to a joyful life. And on, and on, and on…

It's a lie. It's Sprite mixed with Diet Coke.

I climbed the ladder of success to the top only to realize it was leaning against the wrong building.

JEB MCGRUDER, AFTER BEING CONVICTED IN THE WATERGATE SCANDAL

If what the world promises is a sham, then where does the real ginger ale come from? It comes from a relationship with God through Jesus Christ, of course.

Many Christians know this. And as you might suspect, people who don't have a relationship with Jesus aren't aware of the difference between the world's empty promises and actual joy or satisfaction. Our job as followers of Christ is to point out the drastic differences and help them see what true satisfaction and joy can look like.

I have come that they may have life, and have it to the full.
JESUS SPEAKING IN JOHN 10:10B

6
NOT JUST HYPOCRITES ANYMORE

Do you have any idea what people think about you when you tell them that you're a Christian? If you are walking closely with God and have already established some sort of foundational relationship with a friend, they probably have a pretty accurate assumption of what the Bible calls a Christian because you have lived it out well in front of them. However, if you say "Christian" and they really don't know you, their idea of what you are like is most likely a very inaccurate picture of the truth...and things can get awkward.

This makes me sad for a number of reasons:

1. I want people to know the real me.
2. I want others to have a genuine picture of a follower of Christ.
3. Stereotypes of the American Christian are (like other stereotypes) very negative.
4. The stereotype of the American Christian usually comes from media.
5. The people in the media are creating their stereotypes from a few idiots who have represented Christianity very poorly.
6. Idiots are shaping the average American's opinion of Christians.
7. If the average American believes everything they see in the media, they are most likely idiots themselves.

I know that this is a lot to be sad about, but I think you can follow my train of logic pretty well. The truth is, of course, that the reality of who you are as an authentic follower of Jesus will probably never match up with what people think you are based on the aforementioned stereotype. To this day, I have *never* seen a good representation of what I consider to be a genuine Christian in modern American media (movies, television, books). Never.

Now, I know that I haven't seen every single movie or TV show out there, and I surely haven't read every novel or piece of literature, but I'm still on the prowl for an accurate depiction that would make me say, "Yeah, that's what a *real* Bible-believing Christian is like."

Recently, I watched a teen comedy movie with a buddy of mine. Although we thought the movie was incredibly clever and smartly written, we both agreed that, for as smart as the writers were to create the kind of dialogue that they did in the movie, they were completely off target in their depiction of a Christian high schooler (at least any of the Christian high-schoolers that I've ever run in to). The Christians in the movie weren't just hypocrites who loved reveling in their hypocrisy, they were the evil villains who enjoyed heaping judgment, grief, anger and hate on anyone who wasn't as morally "pure" as they were. And to add injury to insult, at the end of the film (spoiler alert) nearly everyone in the movie is redeemed in some way except for the judgmental Christians. When this funny film was over, I found myself sad because of the disgraceful representation of Christ followers.

In early movie history, over-exaggerated representations of people groups were commonplace...especially with ethnic minorities. Today, however, Hollywood is overly sensitive about accurately portraying the reality of people groups in a way that is not stereotypical or offensive—with the exception of Christians.

For some reason, it's open season on Jesus Freaks, who are (in the minds of Hollywood writers) completely out of touch with reality and harshly critical of all people. Does this upset you? Maybe it does, but it's not really the reason I'm telling you all of this.

The reason I point out these stereotypes is to help you understand that many people you encounter will already have a preconceived notion about what you are like because of the groundwork laid by Hollywood and other culture-shapers. When you tell someone that you are a Christian and that you love Jesus, it's very possible that they will believe some things about you that aren't altogether true or even close to reality.

Because of the stereotype, you aren't just a Christian hypocrite anymore; you're a hypocrite who always votes Republican, hates homosexuals, destroys abortion clinics, judges everyone who isn't like you, protests immorality with obnoxious hate-filled handmade signs, and doesn't really listen to anyone...ever. These are some very difficult hurdles to jump over before you can even get to the simple communication of who you really are and what you truly believe.

We now have to work very hard to erase the prejudices brought on by a few bad examples in the past. There's a reason that Jesus said, "Follow me" and not "Follow my followers." Far too often, we set a very bad example for how a Christ-follower should live, but that in itself stands as a highlight of Jesus' magnificent beauty and perfection, right? We are extremely flawed, but Christ chooses to accept and love us anyway. Tim Keller once said that most people in the world are probably our moral superiors, yet the only difference between them and us is that we live in grace as forgiven.[8] We are not forgiven because of what we do, but because of what Jesus Christ has done for us.

The contrast between the truth of authentic Christianity and stereotyped Hollywood Christianity is drastically sharp, and the only way we can prove the world wrong is by showing people the difference, one by one.

I refuse to roll over and accept what the world dishes out about us, but the only way I can fight it is by communicating the truth via living my life in undisputed allegiance to Christ the King while fervently loving others. Yes, it's an uphill battle, but that battle is always worth fighting when we know what's at stake.

7
HIGH SCHOOL POPULARITY AND SKINNY JEANS

Isn't it funny when you look back at pictures of yourself from 5 years ago or more? After the inevitable laugh, your first comment is usually, "Wow, what was I thinking?"

That question is probably in reference to a hairstyle, clothing choice, or accessory faux pas. As I look back on my personal choices of the past, I wonder how I really and truly believed that what I was sporting made me look cool.

It's amazing how quickly style goes out of fashion. Trends in clothing, hair, shoes, etc. are ever-evolving phenomena that bring about embarrassment in a way that no other cultural thing can. For example, one of the best ways to humiliate a friend, coworker, or family member is to publicly show a picture of them when they were in middle school. Adolescence is the moment in time for everyone when we are trying to fit in and be cool. Unfortunately for all of us, though, being cool almost always goes hand-in-hand with the most popular fashion of the day.

Let me continue to illustrate with a more specific trend: skinny jeans. When skinny jeans first arrived on the scene back in the 2007-2008 fashion cycle, I snickered at the fact that high school boys were walking around with peg-leg type denim on their legs, looking as if they would never be able to bend at the knees if asked to sit down. It appeared that I could snap their legs in half if I stared at their jeans hard enough...the boys, along with the jeans, were skinny.

However, 4 months later, I inevitably found myself at the local mall buying multiple pairs of skinny jeans because I thought they actually looked great on me.

Yes, I was completely aware of the fact that my skinny jeans would no longer be fashionably relevant in the future (like, maybe,

3 weeks later), but that didn't change how awesome I thought they were when I paid for them at the register. In a way, my thoughts concerning the jeans are very much the same way that I currently view high school popularity.

For most kids, becoming popular while in high school is the world's greatest achievement, bringing about unfathomable bliss. Popularity is the Holy Grail of social accomplishment and life for a popular kid can quickly decline if something happens to sacrifice public opinion within the walls of the school. It's extremely volatile and can shift like the tide.

But now that I'm out of high school and simply don't care about the inner workings of the social ladder within, I scoff at the idea of placing any kind of value in it. To me, high school popularity is stupid and I really don't see what the big deal is about having something that is based on such shallow pretenses.

But if you asked someone who is actually a student in high school, they would probably disagree with me wholeheartedly. They would talk about the importance of popularity and all of its benefits...then the conversation would undoubtedly veer toward Justin Bieber and Totino's Pizza Rolls.

See, what I'm trying to say is that it's all about your level of personal involvement. Although I believe high school social dynamics are ridiculous, a high school student actually has to experience those dynamics day in and day out. I'm uninvolved, so I don't care, but put me back in my 17-year-old self, and I'll start caring really quickly.

Well, I think the same could be said about the real value that I have for a relationship with God and the emphasis I place on it that someone else might not. Let me explain.

I believe with every fiber of my being that without Christ, I would not experience life in abundance or spend eternity in communion with God in heaven after I die. But if someone else I come across doesn't see their need for a relationship with God, they aren't going to place any value on knowing Him because it simply isn't important to him or her. See what I mean?

Now, it could be for any variety of reasons that they don't see their need: they don't believe in God, they've been put off in the past by Christians or historical Christianity, they don't believe that they're inherently bad, they hate organized religion, etc. But no matter their reason for not seeing their need for Jesus, the truth is that their need exists.

We, as Christians, believe that the ultimate solution to the universal human problem is a personal relationship with God through Jesus Christ. He is the cure for the spiritual cancer that is killing every person on the planet. It doesn't matter if they believe that they are infected with the spiritual cancer or not: its existence is not contingent on their belief.

Christ *is* the remedy to their underlying plight, and the medicine must be dispersed to as many as possible that will take it. Just like my thoughts concerning high school popularity, they may not care about a relationship with God, but unlike adolescent social hierarchies, each and every one of us is very much involved (whether we know it or not) and in need of the remedy.

Being in the world but not of the world requires that you know this. Unless you join a monastery, for the rest of your life you will constantly come in contact with people that don't really see their need for a relationship with God. Even though it may appear that they have it all together and are doing just fine without the Lord in their life, the cancer beneath the surface is killing them. If we gently help people to see the problem, we can then open their eyes to the gracious solution that God offers them in Jesus.

Making them aware of their need is the first step in helping them move toward the solution, and God wants to involve you in that process as much as you are willing. Unlike skinny jeans, a relationship with God will never go out of style, and helping others to see this is the really exciting mission we are a part of as God redeems the world.

8
SLEEPING DISORDERS AND DRUNK PEOPLE

A couple of weeks after I got married, I discovered that my wife would randomly shout out words or short phrases in her sleep.[9] Most of the time that this happened, it didn't bother me at all because the bizarre nature of her erratic vocabulary made me smile. When a person you're laying next to unexpectedly yells, "Leave the umbrella!" you can't help but chuckle as you imagine what they might be dreaming in that moment.

I would tell her the next morning about what she said the night before and then ask if she remembered saying anything at all. She never could recall anything that came out of her mouth and would usually laugh along with me as I described her sleepy verbal escapades.

All of the humor quickly shifted to terror, however, one night during the first year of our marriage. My wife had gone to bed nearly one hour before I did because I had stayed up late to watch a football game that held no interest for her. After the game was over, I shut off the TV and quietly sneaked into the dark bedroom, being very careful not to disturb my slumbering bride. My eyes adjusted to the dark pretty quickly as I walked to my side of the bed and removed my socks. As I was concentrating on taking off my second sock, I heard a rustling in the sheets, so my gaze went to the bed. I saw my wife sit straight up, forming a perfect 90-degree angle. I initially thought that maybe I had woken her up, but that thought swiftly faded when I saw and heard what came next.

She slowly turned her head directly toward me and exclaimed in a firm, yet soft tone, "This is the scary part."

Many things went through my mind at that moment, one of them being, "I think I may have just peed a little." Fear then radiated through my body and I wondered if the person that I had chosen to spend my life with was, in fact, a murderer. I never ran a background check on her during our dating years, and I genuinely believed her when she told me that she loved Jesus…but I've got to tell you, I questioned the validity of her love for God in the moment that night I thought she was going to kill me.

I darted for the lamp on my night table and clicked it on just in case she was holding a knife that I wasn't able to see in the darkness. She looked at me in a daze and then squinted her eyes in angry frustration that I had disrupted her sleep.

"What are you doing?" she asked impatiently, then rolled over and laid her head back down on the pillow.

I stood there for a few seconds, unable to move. The shock eventually wore off and only then did I realize that my wife was not trying to murder me in cold blood, but that she was prone to more demonstrative bouts of harmless sleep talking. I breathed a small sigh of relief, grabbed my pillow, and slept on the couch that night…just in case.

Sleep talking isn't bad at all in the grander scheme of things when it comes to sleeping issues. Everyone has a story to tell about a crazy roommate or spouse who does all kinds of strange things after they close their eyes for the night. In fact, one of my old roommates from my days as a single dude had major freaky sleeping disorders. He once got up from his bed, grabbed a 9 iron from his golf bag in the closet and proceeded to beat the end of his mattress with it because he thought there was a ground hog underneath his sheets. I now pray for his wife's safety every week.

People with sleeping disorders (I've figured out) are a lot like people who are drunk. One minute, they'll love everything about you and want to be all snuggly, and the next minute they can slip into a tirade with enough rage to kill you and destroy everything else in the room that happens to be at arm's length.

The comparison is fair, I think. People who act out in their sleep often have no idea what they are doing and fail to remember their actions the morning after. Drunken people are the same. I know this because I work with college students and often find myself in close proximity to young people prone to party.

Drunkenness on a college campus is commonplace and has been since Prohibition ended in the early 1930s.[10] The idea of "blowing off steam" and "feeling good" supersedes rationality and temporarily fills some very large voids in people's souls. If you, as a mission-minded Christian, are able to see this issue behind the issue, it can be very effective at shaping you into a person who connects with the culture yet avoids immersion in it. Let me explain what I mean…

People don't diagnose their own problems. Someone would never walk into a doctor's office and say, "Doctor, I have a slipped disc between my L4 and L5 vertebrae that is putting pressure on my sciatic nerve, causing radiating pain from my lower back down to the heel of my foot. If you could go ahead and prescribe me some anti-inflammatory medication and get me into physical therapy for a while, I should be feeling better in about six to eight weeks." Uh, no.

They are never going to talk like that, because that's not how people talk. What they will talk about, however, is their symptoms, right? The same thing is true with people's spiritual issues.

No one is ever going to walk up to you and say, "Hey, you're a Christian, right? I feel like there is this gaping hole in my soul that can only be filled by a relationship with God through His Son, Jesus Christ. Can you explain to me in detail how I might accept Him to be my personal Lord and Savior?" Again: uh, no. (Well, if anyone *does* say that to you, it might be a good time to talk with them about the gospel.)

Most likely, people will not talk like that. But they will discuss their symptoms. They'll talk about things like fear, loneliness, anger, and addiction—symptoms of a greater spiritual disease that they are suffering from. They are desperately looking for something to ease the pain in their life, which is why they reach out to things like alcohol, sex, pornography, money, or peer approval. They grasp for ineffective painkillers to assuage the kind of agony that can only be healed by Jesus.

The real question, then, is this: Do you believe that you have what people are really looking for? Do you believe that the only thing that can really satisfy a person's thirst is a loving relationship with God through Jesus Christ?

If you do, you will begin to understand not only where people are coming from when they talk about their symptoms, but you'll also be able to help address their real needs with an actual satisfying solution…one that isn't hollow, temporary, or unfulfilling.

It may feel awkward to engage with someone's issues on that deep of a level at first, but people truly are longing for a connection in life. And just think: you might be the privileged person to guide them from their daily struggles of practical pain to that satisfying relationship with God that they've been looking for their whole life.

9
THE WOOL OVER OUR EYES

I wanna have a good time and enjoy my Jack...sit back and watch the women get drunk as hell, so I can wake up in the morning with a story to tell.
LUDACRIS, *GET BACK*

You have to consider the possibility that God does not like you. He never wanted you. In all probability, He hates you...we don't need Him. [Forget] salvation! [Forget] redemption! We are God's unwanted children? So be it!
BRAD PITT AS TYLER DURDEN, *FIGHT CLUB* (EDITED BY ME)[11]

Let me give you a little inside information about God. God likes to watch. He's a prankster. Think about it. He gives man instincts. He gives you this extraordinary gift, and then what does He do? I swear for His own amusement, his own private, cosmic gag reel, He sets the rules in opposition. It's the goof of all time. Look but don't touch. Touch, but don't taste. Taste, don't swallow. And while you're jumpin' from one foot to the next, what is he doing? He's laughin'!...He's a SADIST! He's an absentee landlord! Worship that? NEVER!
AL PACINO AS JOHN MILTON, *THE DEVIL'S ADVOCATE*

The bigger the lie, the more it will be believed.
JOSEPH GOEBBELS, ADOLF HITLER'S PROPAGANDA MINISTER IN NAZI GERMANY

There is something inherently attractive about a lie that draws us in like an insect to the light. Sometimes I wonder why that is. Maybe it's because most of us are skeptics by nature and really don't want to believe the truth that's obviously in front of our faces. Maybe it's because most of us are stupid and we can't tell the difference between the truth and a lie. Or maybe it's because we all have a very real enemy in Satan who loves to fool us into believing certain variances of the truth mixed with lies (like a Banana Berry Smoothie from Jamba Juice laced with cyanide).

I have a tendency to believe that it's probably all of those and more. But maybe it doesn't really matter *why* we are attracted to lies. Perhaps it's more about the fact that lies are capable of destroying anything and everything around us, including the very condition of our souls.

From little white lies to faith-crushing big ones, deception is a powerful influence that has pulled the wool over humanity's eyes and tricked us into believing all sorts of untruths, like certain evils are no big deal, people can save themselves, and if God even exists, He either hates us or doesn't really want to be personally involved in our lives. And with those kinds of results, I'd say that's an awful lot of power that can put a damper of intimidation over the efforts of truth to shine through darkness. But that's exactly what the truth does—it shines brightly to destroy the darkness of lies.

In a fallen world, it doesn't take much to plant a seed of darkness and watch it grow. The Enemy, our sinful nature, and the world[12] all have an active role in this process, to the point that it feels impossible to spread the truth with any kind of significant influence. In the short run, darkness can easily choke out any hope for a glimmer of good to break forth and wash all of the gloom away.

The suicide note written and left by the jazz-age cartoonist Ralph Barton provides evidence to this:

> *I have had few difficulties, many friends, great successes; I have gone from wife to wife, and from house to house, visited countries of the world, but I am fed up with inventing devices to fill up 24 hours of the day.*

The lies told by the Enemy would have you believe that there is no hope. God is not present in your life and there's really no reason for Him to be present because He hates you anyway. You might as well be as corrupt as possible because that is the only kind of medicine able to numb the pain of an existence on this wretched planet.

These lies are powerful and influential; they burrow under the skin of our conscience and fester like a disease. They distract us so that our hearts become hypnotized with despair…kind of like the way Sarah McLachlan's early musical work did to the feelings of American college women back in the mid '90s.

But in the battle between darkness and light, light always wins out. It is always able to cut through the anguish-soaked blackness that can engulf a person's life. Whenever darkness decides to step up and go toe-to-toe with the light, light always delivers the knockout punch that makes its enemy drop to the floor. The result: hope.

Why? Ultimately, because darkness is no match for the light, ever. The world would have you believe that evil is the dominant force in the universe, unable to be shackled or contained by the feeble attempts of God or His human followers, but the world (once again) is wrong. God has been and will forever remain the victor in the battle, which will be proven once and for all when evil is destroyed for all time (see the book of Revelation…all of it).

Now, you might say, "This is all fine and good, but the end of the world is probably a long way off and I would kindly like to know how to deal with the lies of the world in a practical way today as I wrestle with life's choices."

Good point, and spoken like a true American. I'm a practical guy too, and I always prefer getting to the guts of what it all means rather than dealing with the uncertainty of the theoretical.

Well, like with many other things, the rubber actually meets the road in the daily walk of life. As American Christians, we are constantly looking to the end result of the journey for answers instead of what the journey itself means. Lord help me, but I have to say that Miley Cyrus got it right when she sang, "It's all about the climb."

Life is lived in the present, not in what we want to happen in the future. If you think that a formula can be plugged into your life now in order to produce a certain desirable end result, all of a sudden you have become a math problem to be solved, and God doesn't work that way. He isn't calculatingly sterile and He isn't comfortably convenient. He values relationships and those happen in the context of moment-by-moment interactions on the journey of your life.

Every day will present you with opportunities to reject the lies of Satan and this world or to be charmed by them, and each day will be defined by that rejection or acceptance. If you swallow and ingest those lies on a continual basis, you will easily fall under the alluring spell of the world's fiction and find yourself blinded like so many others around you. You'll start to think that your existence is only about pleasure, that God doesn't love you, that He is a cruel "absentee landlord," and He may not even exist at all.

Don't swallow it. I know that it's a difficult journey, but God walks the path with us. If you don't believe me, open up your bible and read the gospels. Jesus chose to step out of the ultimate comfort in the universe to walk beside filthy human beings and show them how much God wanted to be with them. He offered redemption to them and He offers it to you today. Evil is screaming at you to turn away from the truth and buy into what it has to offer, but as succulent as its fruit may look, it will quickly turn to ash.

It is so important to identify the lies that you are bent toward believing and replace them with the truth of what God has to offer. The consequences of your actions define the very identity of who you are now and who you will become in the future.

Someone very wise once told me, "First you make your choices, and then your choices make you." My advice is to hold on to that proverbial slogan and run with it each day.

10
WHITE (AND ORANGE) TRASH

During my junior year of college at VA Tech, I shared an apartment with three other dudes that I considered to be some of my best friends in the world. And they certainly were. Not only did we live together, but we also spent social time together, frequently talked with one another, and even visited each other's families on occasion during school breaks. I loved these guys and I was incredibly thankful that God had brought them into my life during my first few years as a Christian.

All that being said, some of them had a few behavioral patterns that clashed a bit with my ideal way of living. I'm not talking about personality flaws or anything like that; I'm just referring to the general lack of concern for the overall cleanliness of our place. You see, I have a tendency to be somewhat OCD when it comes to tidiness.

Yes, I recognize that this is an abnormal trait for an American male (especially during the college years), but I have no qualms about waving my cleanliness banner high and proud in the face of anyone that might challenge it with shallow mockery. And as you might have deduced by now, some of those unapologetic challengers were the men I chose to share living space with those many years ago.

The specific area of our apartment that drew my attention on a regular basis was our kitchen. Now I'm not going to lie and say that I was perfect at cleaning every single dish that I used as soon as I was done with it, but I was intentional about making sure that my dirty dishes would not pile up because of continuing neglect. My roommates did not share this same passion when it came to the dishes in the sink, nor for that matter, the trashcan that was nestled snuggly in the corner next to the fridge. They would frequently allow the garbage to build up in the can so much that it would overflow down onto the open floor space where there was plenty of room for things to pile up.

The most noteworthy of occasions that this happened began in late October and ran all the way up through Christmas break. That's right, there was trash piled up in our kitchen for over two months. It all started with a communal lazy streak of allowing it to build for about two or three weeks, but then quickly morphed into an agreed upon insurmountable obstacle that none of us wished to face. The act of creating a mini-landfill in the corner became a kind of contest to see how long we could actually go without (as we put it) "allowing the garbage to win." This was the *only* reason that I allowed this preposterous idea to proceed…because it turned into a competition. What can I say? I'm a dude and I love to compete.

Day after day, week after week, we continued to add to the growing hill of rubbish that became known as "Mt. Trashmore." It got to the point that when we wanted to throw something away, we wouldn't even have to step into the kitchen anymore. We would simply walk past the room's entryway and blindly chuck our trash into the corner without looking. You might think that this is completely gross (and you're probably right), but in a way, it was also completely awesome.

Well, Christmas break finally arrived and we gave in. Everybody joined in and we all disposed of the legendary Mt. Trashmore as a team. It took nearly an hour to do so because the discarded pumpkin we had bought for Halloween was rotted out on the bottom and when we lifted it up, its base turned to liquid and splashed down all over the kitchen floor leaving a huge orange mess. It wasn't a pretty cleanup, but we did it.

When I think about or retell this story, the parallel that comes to my mind is the way that people sometimes think about themselves. We all have so much garbage in our lives that we allow to build up over time. It grows and grows to the point that it looks almost impossible to clean up and scary to even go near. Here's the typical line of thinking: Because of all this horrible clutter that has clogged up my soul, I am not worthy of love, acceptance, or forgiveness. If Christ (who promises love, acceptance and forgiveness) were to enter into a relationship with me, I would need to remove all of that crap in my life before I could take a step toward him. But because of the trash hill's size, I am overwhelmed with the very idea of addressing it.

This belief is not uncommon. I have talked with so many people who have asked the question, "Why would God want to love and forgive me? I'm such a bad person." Even in today's self-esteem driven culture, people are very much in the business of beating themselves up and neglecting God because of their past moral or spiritual failures.

Our responsibility as mission-minded believers is to identify this false belief in the lives of others and replace it with the truth of the gospel. Never once does God ask us to "get your stuff together and then I'll be willing to accept you." We are not asked to be clean before we can be forgiven. The good news of Scripture tells us:

Though your sins are like scarlet, they shall be as white as snow; though they are red as crimson, they shall be like wool.
ISAIAH 1:18

And:

For by works of the law no human being will be justified in his sight…
ROM. 3:20, ESV

God meets us right where we are at, piled up garbage and all, and exclaims to us, "Even though you are dirty and sinful, I will make you as white as the snow. You cannot work to be justified in my sight by doing good things. A relationship with me comes through faith alone by my grace."[13]

This is the true message that must be communicated to anyone and everyone that we know. Once they begin to see the extreme contrast between the truth of the gospel and their own false beliefs, they will be willing to hand their trash-laden lives over to God by the power of the Holy Spirit.

Communicate this news well and communicate it often because it is the greatest message that history has ever known. It's not people's own responsibility to take the trash out; it's God's.

PART TWO

THINGS THAT GET IN YOUR WAY

INTRODUCTION: OBSTACLES

Hazing is a fun way to show a new employee that they are not welcome or liked.
DWIGHT SCHRUTE, *THE OFFICE*

I'm a military brat. If you're unfamiliar with that term, it basically means that I grew up in a military family (specifically, the Air Force) where we moved to a new location every few years. Growing up with that kind of lifestyle as the norm was difficult to say the least, but the experience of constantly moving, time and time again, shaped me into the person that I am today and for that I am extremely grateful.

Because moving became routine after (on average) every two years or so, quickly making new friends in each new environment was a large part of the adaptation process. And although I understood this concept quite well, I was a natural introvert and fairly inflexible when it came to pioneering new life adventures. Consequently, the common parental adage of "go make some new friends" was a rather large obstacle for me.

We all know that kids can be quite cruel, and because I frequently wore the unpopular label of "new kid," I became all too familiar with the notion of uncaring fellow students. (This is a polite way of saying that kids can be jerks.) One particular memory that springs to the forefront of my mind occurred during the beginning of my sophomore year of high school.

My freshman year was spent in Stafford, Virginia, surrounded by familiarity because of the rare four-year stint that my dad spent stationed at the Pentagon in Washington, D.C. New orders meant a new home, so we packed up and headed off to Montgomery, Alabama, where I found myself as one of only two new kids at a small private Christian school, populated predominantly by white rich kids that enjoyed torturing almost anyone who showed any sign of weakness.

Cut and zoom to metaphorical target indelibly printed on my face.

One particular day, after two weeks of sitting with the other new guy during lunch, he was invited to join the popular dudes at their table, which left me literally by myself at the end of a long cafeteria table, alone with my PB & J. Now, ask any high schooler and they'll be able to tell you that there is no worse time to fly solo than at lunch time. I was horrified. In fact, even now as I recount this story, I feel the same knot in my stomach that I felt that day.

One of the nicer girls in the school eventually extended to me a merciful invitation to join her and her friends for the remainder of lunchtime, and I breathed a small sigh of relief as I joined them.

Well, the reason I'm sharing this with you is not to make you feel sorry for me (although you probably do), but to illustrate to you that there are a myriad of stumbling blocks in life that will constantly stand in your way and prevent you from achieving your various desired outcomes. In that moment during my sophomore year in the cafeteria, all I wanted was a friend to sit with so that I could feel accepted in a new school. The obstacle was there that day and it took some time and effort, but I eventually overcame those challenges and found a few friends that I enjoyed my meals with in the lunchroom as the year went on.

Similarly, there will constantly be hurdles for you to jump over in the process of figuring out what it means to be *in* the world but not *of* the world. Some of those barricades will come from the world itself in the form of preconceived notions about who you are as a Christian. It can be an uphill battle for you to vanquish those prejudices over time in the midst of a very cynical society. Other obstacles will undoubtedly come from within you, be it from the haunting of past failures, current sin issues, fear, or even self-loathing.

While staring those impediments in the eye, take heart that Jesus Christ has dealt with all of this permanently by His work on the cross. No, it may not always be easy. And yes, most of us are carrying a lot of external and internal baggage, but the power of Christ's death and resurrection ultimately prevails over the very real issues you face as a human being. You must believe this as truth.

The challenges are, of course, quite real (like my solo lunchroom experience that day), but overcoming them simply begins with the investigation of there existence. Being made aware of the obstacles in your path tips the scales in your favor as you wrestle with what it means to be a Christian in the world but not of the world.

11
ALL THE SINGLE LADIES (AND DUDES)

Deep down, I know that marriage won't solve all of my problems...but even deeper down than that, I know marriage will solve all of my problems.
SHELBY ABBOTT, 2002

There is a common obsession among the young and old that is capable of monopolizing someone's time, attention, and heart. It is written about in song, acted out in television and movies, chatted about on the web, talked about on the phone and murmured about in office break rooms. It is capable of making the hardest of personalities malleable, and the most cynical of attitudes idealistic. It can make the heart soar with delight and optimism yet it can leave a person dejected and completely downtrodden for months. I'm not talking about the Dairy Queen Blizzard; I'm talking about love.

When I was a single guy back in college, I thought that women could be ruthless...just completely without 'ruth' altogether. The reason was that most of the ladies I encountered said that they wanted a sensitive guy—someone they could snuggle and cry with while watching any movie on the Lifetime Network. Sensitivity was "in" when I was a college student, and I found out very quickly that what women said wasn't necessarily what they wanted. I know this because I actually *was* a sensitive man. Trust me though; being a sensitive guy doesn't get you a girlfriend. Being sensitive gets you laughed at. For example, during my freshman year of college, I wanted to show this girl I was crushing out on (some call this "Diggin' her chili") how sensitive I could be, so I allowed myself to cry in front of her. When I did, I figured that this would be my opportunity to communicate the kind of depth I had as a man. Uh, no.

Needless to say, it backfired on me. She immediately got all awkward and shifty-eyed. She took a few steps away from me and said, "Uh, could you please stop that. You're making me feel uncomfortable. Please take me home." I never tried that approach with a girl ever again.

Well, I'm married now and I'm thankful that I don't have to be a part of the dating scene at all anymore. I can honestly say that I have zero desire to step back into that world...but my reasons for that might be different than what you might think.

The main reason that I don't want to go back to the Single Shelby Era (or SSE) is because, quite frankly, I'm somewhat ashamed of the person I used to be. Not because I was a player or anything like that. And not even because I regret how I treated any of the women that I chose to go out with. I'm ashamed of the person I used to be because I found myself constantly obsessing about what the girl in question thought of me.

See, in the SSE, I wrestled a lot with insecurity and self-scrutiny to the point that my world would rise and fall under the opinion of what the girl whose chili I was diggin' thought about me that day. Does she still like me today? Am I a good enough boyfriend? Why didn't she call me this morning? Is she mad at me? Bored with me? Annoyed by me? Not attracted to me anymore? It was endless and exhausting.

Because of my grand insecurity, I inevitably got to the point that I would become overzealous in my pursuit of a certain girl and she would back away because I smothered her. Honestly, I just didn't know when to quit. It wouldn't be a stretch to say that I was lame.

Now, does it make me sad that this is the type of guy I used to be? Yes, of course...but on the bright side, when I talk to current singles who are dealing with a personality similar to what I used to be, I can dispense some pretty great advice on how to handle the lame and needy guy or girl.

What changed in me, though, is that I finally made a decision to grow up and let my relationship with Christ be my security. Sure, that sounds simple, but it really is the truth. When I finally resolved to truly stop the quest for seeking satisfaction in the opinion of the opposite sex, my whole perspective on who I was as a person became different.

I didn't need to feed off of the approval of girls to help me define my self worth because I knew that I was infinitely valuable in the site of God. He gave up His Son for me, for crying out loud!

When I look back on the guy I used to be, I have to laugh. In fact, whenever I speak to large groups, most of my humorous illustrations about relationships are plucked directly from my own misguided attempts at love. I was incredibly juvenile, but man, I was funny.

What is not funny, however, is that the mistakes I made for many years are now carbon-copied by single men and women all the time today. In numerous cases, the blunder of choice is "Opposite Sex Obsession." And it exists now for the same reason it existed back when I had it—insecurity.

The constant need to be with someone or liked by someone or thought of by someone stems directly from the sin of placing your self worth or approval in the hands of the opposite sex instead of God. And when this happens, the manifestation of that sin often presents itself in an overzealous obsession. Not only do your thoughts about having a boyfriend or girlfriend rule your life, but they also lead you to do and say things that no ordinary person in their right mind would do or say.

I have literally heard stories of guys and girls on a first date talking about what they want to name their children and where they want to get married. You might think that this is funny, right? Well, I agree with you, but is it unhealthy? Or worse, is it ungodly?

I don't think I can answer those last two with certainty, but what I can say is that an obsession with the opposite sex definitely acts as an idol in the hearts of many single men and women today. They bow down to it and worship every day, thinking that marriage is the holy grail of life solutions.

"Nothing could be better than marriage because when it finally happens for me, all of my problems will go away." Many of you are buying into this line of thinking. Well, I can tell you that I waited in that line, got to the front, scanned my ticket, and crossed over to the other side while giving the SSE the proverbial finger. I can truly tell you that I love being married, but at the same time, I truly regret my attitude before I got there.

I literally wasted so much time worshiping the idol of Opposite Sex Obsession and I wish I hadn't bowed down. My heart could have been in such a better place each day if I would have given it completely to Christ and trusted that He would not only be my fulfillment for that day, but that if He so desired, He could lead me to the right person to spend my life with. Unfortunately, I didn't trust Him to do that and I consequently took it upon myself to find the right one. And I failed again and again and again...and again.

If your heart is longing for life with another person more than a life with Christ, I can promise that you will end up being disappointed in not only the human relationship you will get, but also in your perspective of God's involvement in your life. A person's love can never adequately substitute for the love of God through Jesus Christ. It's not possible because people can't love that much and God can't be that uninvolved.

When I finally let go of my petty idol worship and yielded to God's call to actively depend on Him and diligently surrender to Him, my heart was finally ready for my future mate...and we started dating 3 months later. (Just an aside—I treated her differently than any other girl I had dated before. Not obsessive, needy or clingy. I didn't push too hard. I gave her space. I placed my relationship with God at the forefront of my life and encouraged her to do the same. A totally different process and outcome!)

Being in the world but not of the world means living your life in contrast to the norm while maintaining a sincere connection to those that don't follow Christ. If we act like we are no different than any other person out there in our relationships with the opposite sex, what kind of attraction will others have to a relationship to Christ?

A healthy and godly approach to singleness and relationships will always stand in sharp contrast to the ugliness of the world's way of doing it. All we have to do is consistently choose God's approach to illustrate the dichotomy for people to see. And once they see it, they will long to know what really lies behind it.

12
AWKWARD ANNIE'S

In my opinion, Christians can be really funny; and most of the time, not in the good way. Not funny "ha-ha," but more like funny "weird." As I've said before many times in this book, more often than not, any Christian that you run into is probably going to be somewhat awkward in a very obvious way. Other times, their awkwardness doesn't expose itself until something triggers it...but don't worry, it's probably there.

I say this because I've been a Christian since my freshman year of college and I've spent a lot of my life surrounded by them...or should I say, "us." Christians are very fond of the certain lifestyle that we choose to build and we want to make sure that others (non-Christians) are aware of that lifestyle. We tend to act like show-offs, displaying our faith/lifestyle on obnoxious bumper stickers or highway advertisement signage. We are bold, but only when it's safe.

When *The Passion of the Christ* came out, American Christians everywhere were peeing their pants with excitement. We were all super stoked about the fact that we had Mel Gibson on our team. Knowing that the creator of *Braveheart* and star of *Lethal Weapon 3* was now our advocate, we walked around with the arrogance of a graduating senior from UVA (sorry, I meant to say *fourth year*[14]). And because his Jesus movie was such a hit, Christians were approaching Mel for interviews, speaking engagements, and book endorsements just so that we could make sure that all the pagans out there knew that Mel Gibson's name was written in the Lamb's Book of Life. We reveled in it and cherished the time we had with him as our spokesperson.

Then, of course, Mel Gibson went crazy and every American Christian felt like the Nike Corporation after Tiger Woods got busted for being a philanderer. You could almost hear the collective sigh of frustration around every church narthex refreshment table. We were angry and we were downtrodden. But then like a giant super ball, we bounced back and moved on. The hunt continues to this day for our next Hollywood conversion representative (I'm hoping it's J.J. Abrams).

When other opportunities arise for us to show off our Christianity to the world, we love to take them. This assures that our Spiritual Yummies get as much airtime on the local news as possible. In case you were wondering, a Spiritual Yummy is the sound that a Christian will make when they agree with you about a certain spiritual comment, prayer, or opinion. It's the *"mmmm"* sound that signifies our acceptance of the spiritual case submitted. Sometimes, the *"mmmm"* can be followed up with an even more reassuring *"mmm-hmm"* or sometimes a verbal "praise God", but one never can tell. These Spiritual Yummies set us apart from the normal crowd, yet they help anyone to see just how mingled into society we actually are...we like that people know this.

My opinion, however, is that these kinds of Christian things don't really make us any cooler. In fact, I think they really have the opposite effect—they make us more awkward...and that's usually not a good thing. Most people have an intrinsic sense of knowing when something gets weird, and they usually try to either eliminate the awkward feeling or simply run away when it shows up.

I'll give you an example. A few years ago, I had the chance to go on a "creative date" with a number of other friends. A creative date is basically a large group date that is typically theme-based and makes Christians even more strange. In this case, the girls had prepared the date for a group of us guys to participate in and it really is one date that will go down in the record books for me as completely memorable.

Being the gentlemen that we were, we arrived promptly at the time we were told to show up. When we got there, the door to the residence was labeled with a piece of paper that read "Awkward Annie's." I hesitantly looked at the guy next to me and said, "This outta be good." To this day, I'm still not sure if I was right or wrong.

After we knocked, the door opened, revealing a long line of girls in single file down the entryway. All of them were smiling and saying hi at the same time. The first girl in line shouted, "Come in!" and gave one of my buddies a big hug. All of us filed in, one at a time, as each girl reached out and gave every one of us a side-hug. When I reached the end of the overwhelming line of females, the last girl in line said, "Smile!" and quickly snapped a digital picture of me by myself. The uncomfortable night had just begun.

The evening was earmarked with wonderfully horrible occurrences that would make even the cast of *The Office* cringe. I quickly discovered that one of the girls dressed up like she was pregnant and would respond with anger anytime someone asked her about it. Dinner was served to us without forks or spoons and the beverages we consumed were poured into cereal bowls instead of cups. After our meal, we played a large group game of "spin the bottle", only to have the actual kisses replaced with Hershey's chocolate. One of the girls intentionally spilled a drink in my buddy's lap "on accident" and made a huge spectacle of being sorry for what she had done. Most of the women would refuse to engage in conversation with us so that the awkward silence meter would continually be pushed higher and higher as the evening went on. I'm telling you—the night was awkward.

All in all, I think that we as the guys were really good sports. My buddy, Justin, even got into the act with the girls and said that caricature henna tattoo on his arm translated into the ... for *pervert*. It was fun.

But again, that evening will be indelibly written in my memory because the raw emotion of awkwardness I experienced went hand-in-hand with the actual events. The girls truly accomplished their goal of making us feel awkward, and even though I enjoyed it, I don't think I would ever want to go through that date again.

Why? Well, like I said before, people naturally flee from awkward situations. We don't like to feel socially uncomfortable and will probably do anything to avoid it.

Consequently, I believe this is one of the major reasons that Christians don't want to bring up anything about God or Jesus when they engage with someone in conversation. You know the rule: if you want a happy group environment, don't bring up politics or religion.

But let me retort with this: why does a conversation about God have to be an awkward one? Tell me, what is awkward about engaging with a loving God that accepts you because of grace and not works? What is awkward about living a life that is free from the guilt and slavery of sin? What's awkward about being personally involved in the greatest story of redemption ever told?

The answer is "nothing," so that leads us to believe that the source of awkwardness can only come from the delivery of the Christian message or our own preconceived beliefs that people do not want to hear what we have to say. And both of these conclusions are laid directly at the feet of the Christian himself. The problem lies not in the message, but with the messenger.

Appropriate delivery of the gospel message is all about understanding appropriate communication. It's about having discernment to know when to speak and when not to speak, what to say and what not to say, gauging whether or not the person you're talking with is tracking with you or off in La-La Land; those kinds of things.

When you talk with others about your relationship with God, are you being "them-centered"? It's always our default to focus on ourselves when we are presenting something, but the real wisdom and effectiveness comes when we can let go of how *we* look and concentrate on the *listener*. This way, we are able to make small adjustments in the actual content we present and tailor it to the way that they process and receive information. It might be very surprising to hear this, but Communication 101 is essentially the best way to rid a God-conversation of awkwardness.

Now, let's deal with the preconceived belief that people just don't want to hear the message. I will say that sometimes this can be true, and if it is, you'll be able to tell almost immediately based on body language or actual verbal confirmation that they aren't comfortable with the way the conversation is going. If that's the case, simply move on to some other topic.

However, I've found that a lot of people really love to share their opinions about spiritual things and enjoy listening to what you believe about who God is and what He is like. If we preemptively destroy any possibility of a conversation about the gospel because we think they'll be turned off, the fault is ours, not theirs. I realize that finding that perfect moment in a conversation to inject the gospel can be difficult, but the more you try it, the more accustomed you will be at finding a natural transition.

Like a lot of stuff in life, this isn't a formulaic science, but an art—maybe even a dance. Hear me out: you can learn the steps by practicing, but the beauty and flow of the dance happens when you get in sync with the music and the person you're dancing with... and it just works. But if you assume that the person doesn't even want to talk with you about God, the dance is over before it even had a chance to begin. Don't make that mistake.

Awkwardness shouldn't be something that prevents us from speaking up about what we believe. It is something that can be easily dealt with if you are prepared. That doesn't mean that awkwardness will never show its ugly head in your conversations, but if it does show up, at least you'll have a great story to tell and something funny to laugh about with your other awkward friends.

Mmmm.

13
CONVERSATIONS WITH BRIAN

Brian is the name of the fictitious uber-Christian that I sporadically converse with in my mind. He represents the stereotypical pushy, defensive, insensitive Christian. You probably wouldn't like him. Brian is always up-front about the way he feels and he adamantly defends his Christian viewpoint on all subjects, regardless of how I may react to them. He is unapologetic about his beliefs, and he will not hesitate to point out the flaws in my life when I choose to be transparent enough to show my true colors.

Shelby: If you had a choice to go see a movie in the theater, would you typically pick an action film or a comedy?

Brian: That depends on what each of the films was rated.

Shelby: Okay, let's say they're both rated the same. Both of them are PG-13. Would you pick a PG-13 action movie or a PG-13 comedy movie?

Brian: Out of the question. I wouldn't go see either.

Shelby: Why?

Brian: Because I won't subject myself to the kind of movie that is evil enough to earn a PG-13 rating by the MPAA. I'd rather watch neither. If I really desire to see some action, I have every season of *Walker: Texas Ranger* on DVD to watch here at home, and if I want a really good laugh, there are plenty of funny Tim Hawkins videos I can look up online. This is all much more wholesome entertainment than that perverse stuff shown in theaters nowadays.

Shelby: Fine, fine…forget I mentioned it.

Brian: Forgotten. I forgive you. I choose to extend grace to you even though you are a rotten sinner.

It is somewhat difficult for me to rationalize with the different parts of my personality that superficially clash with one another. I'm not talking about the deep parts of my soul that deal with the real esoteric issues of life; I'm talking about the tiny and inconsequential day-to-day things that make me ask myself silly things like, "Why must I first eat all the oat pieces in a bowl of Lucky Charms before moving on to the marshmallows?" The answer to that, of course, is that I want to save the marshmallows for last because I love the way they taste in milk without the annoying hindrance of unequally delicious oat pieces…but I digress.

My conversations with Brian represent the various aspects of (a) who I currently am and (b) the person I once was as a hyper-religious young man. They are a small slice of the thought process that can be plucked from my mind, slowed down, and then dissected to help you understand the minutiae of opinions I hold because of the influences from my past, other people, and self-expectations.

Is Brian really me from the past? Yes and no. *Yes*, I used to be an exceptional rule-follower who took pride in being holier than others. But *no*, because I really don't think I was ever that exasperating.

Shelby: I've come to the conclusion that there are no natural blue foods.

Brian: What do you mean?

Shelby: I mean there are no foods that exist in nature that are truly the color blue.

Brian: What about blue berries?

Shelby: They're not really blue, they're purple.

Brian: Okay, what about blue corn chips?

Shelby: Not blue. They're really more black.

Brian: Fine. How about blue raspberry? That's definitely blue.

Shelby: I said foods that occur *naturally*. The last time I checked, you couldn't grow blue raspberries to puree into a syrup and pour all over snow cones.

Brian: Well, it doesn't really matter to me if a food is any particular color, just as long as it is organic.

Shelby: Listen, we've had this conversation so many times and I'm getting sick of it. Yes, I think buying organic is a responsible way to eat, but I just can't do it with everything. I'd really prefer to eat healthier in every way, but I'd also prefer to continue living in my house without a second mortgage. Organic products are too expensive.

Brian: Yes they are, but the bible says that our body is a temple, thus we should treat it the best way that we know how. You should probably just pray about it. And when you do, ask yourself this question: "What would Jesus eat?"

Brian is pretentious and pious. He loves to make a show out of the fact that he can bring God into any situation. And if I don't give the appropriate value to the Lord's involvement in the mix of all life issues, I should probably check myself and re-evaluate my motivations. In addition to his constant holy irritation, Brian has other flaws. They are flaws that aren't as easy to spot, but I promise that they are there because I see signs of them in myself every now and again.

Shelby: I've been thinking lately that I don't necessarily talk to enough people about my faith.

Brian: Well, you should. I think Jesus would want that.

Shelby: Maybe I'll go talk to the buddy I've been thinking about sharing with right now.

Brian: Really? Why now?

Shelby: No time like the present, right? It's been something that I've been meaning to do for a while now so I should just get off my butt and go talk to him. Let's go.

Brian: Well, I really can't go right now.

Shelby: What for?

Brian: Well, I was just in the middle of starting a mental volunteer list of people that I wanted to challenge at being more active in the church, and after that I was going to finish up the chapter I was reading in *Stuff Christians Like*. It's a busy time for me right now. I'll tell you what, though…I'll go ahead and put him on my list to pray for when I do my devotionals tomorrow morning.

For all of Brian's religious lessons on life, the truth of the matter is that he is somewhat of a coward. Sure, he's bold about hacking away at my selfish motivations in the little details of my days and nights, but when push comes to shove, he hides under his bubble of Christianity because it is safe for him.

Safety is a very high value of Brian's. In fact, it may be his most important priority. When moments arise for Brian to show me how to do the right thing, he will not hesitate to step in and speak up. Still, for all of his verbose diatribes on my religious shortcomings,

he is afraid to say anything about his faith whe
presented to him.

This irks me.

I feel like every time I have the pure motiva
my faith to someone, Brian is there to dissuade me from doing it by coming up with an overabundance of excuses to avoid it at all costs.

Is it as if I am experiencing my very own Tyler Durden moment when these fake conversations exist? After reading the last several pages, you're probably ready to give a resounding "YES!" But keep in mind that I haven't yet resorted to beating myself up and as much as I know, I haven't spawned an underground boxing circuit.

However, the fact remains that part of me is very comfortable with being very comfortable as a protected Christian, calling fouls from the sidelines but completely unwilling to suit up and hit the playing field to make a real difference in the game.

Rules are easy to follow if your motivation is to look better than others around you. But when the thought of your reputation being tainted in front of those others whose opinions you value so highly becomes a reality, the core of your true values are revealed.

John 12:42-43 illustrates this better than anything I could ever come up with:

> *Yet at the same time many even among the leaders believed in him. But because of the Pharisees they would not confess their faith for fear they would be put out of the synagogue; for they loved praise from men more than praise from God.*

Because of the value that these new believers had for the praise of the Pharisees, they neglected to confess their faith. People's opinions became more crucial than God's.

Now, I always have a tendency to read pieces of Scripture like this and say, "Stupid idiots. They shouldn't be afraid of the lousy [illegible]isees. What a bunch of sissies." But I have no room to talk [b]ecause I long for the approval of people more than the approval of God every day that I breathe. It's easy to sit and read a story in the comfort of my home and pass judgment on the believers that were afraid of sharing their faith way back then. But how often do I shy away from the very same situations when God sovereignly ushers them into my life today? Answer: almost every time.

But this should not be.

Brian exists not only in me, but in every American believer. He may take on a slightly different personality for you than he does for me, but he's there in your mind like a splinter. Ignoring him in the watershed moments when God wants you to confess your faith is a daunting task. But let this be your motivation: praise from our loving Father is far more to be treasured than the fickle opinions of humanity.

Shelby: I'm fairly certain that white Christians' favorite thing to make fun of are other white Christians...usually via blogging.

Brian: I can't blame them. We are a hilarious subset of the culture at large.

14
I DISLIKE GLITTER AND WebMD

Glitter might be one of the worst inventions in all of human history. You might think that I'm joking, but I'm as serious about this as Darth Vader was about turning Luke to the dark side in *The Empire Strikes Back.*[15]

If I ever run for office, the bedrock of my campaign strategy won't be to balance the budget or fix the health care crisis. It will be the push for complete and total annihilation of the glitter department in the American greeting card industry.

Everybody's got their one ultimate archenemy: Superman has Lex Luthor, the Red Sox have the Yankees, the democrats have Rush Limbaugh, Chuck Klosterman has Coldplay[16], and I have glitter. I once heard a comedian say that glitter was "the herpes virus of the crafting world…it just spreads everywhere." I couldn't agree more.

Three years ago, I got a birthday card in the mail that had glitter on it and when I opened it, it was like a New Year's Eve party exploded all over my living room. There was glitter *everywhere.* Glitter on the carpet, glitter between the couch cushions, glitter on my shoes, glitter in my hair, glitter on my pillow…I was finding glitter scattered around every part of my life for months after I opened that despicable Hallmark birthday wish.

No joke: three weeks went by after I thought that I had finally gotten rid of it all, and I found a speck of glitter in a fresh pair of underpants when I was folding the laundry. Time froze as I held that contaminated pair of boxer shorts and I imagined a movie camera, rigged to a boom operator, zooming in close to my face and whirling around my entire body while slowly moving up toward the ceiling. I closed my eyes, extended both fists to the air (one clenching the underwear, of course) and let out a prolonged and dramatic, "Nooooooo!" Needless to say, I now let my wife open any and every greeting card that comes into our home. And if one happens to be infected with glitter, she is immediately forced to throw it in the trashcan and wash her hands in the basement utility sink not once, not twice, but thrice times. I think you're hearing what I'm saying by now, right?

Although my disdain for glitter runs strong through my veins, there are a number of other things in this world that also cause me to grumble. I'm a sinful pessimist by nature and things like traffic, crooked window shades, pieces of white fuzz on a black shirt, anything with Bill Maher's name attached to it, the Greyhound bussing system, and men's swim trunks with the sewn-in mesh tighty-whitey underwear all rub me the wrong way...sometimes literally. But from the long list of things I dislike, I'm going to focus for a few moments on the website, WebMD.

The good people over at WebMD, bless their hearts[17], have caused a significant amount of distress in my life over the last few years. I know that this is not their intention, of course, but the best intentions of a public medical website really have nothing to do with the fact that I constantly misdiagnose all of my illnesses based upon the information spit out at me when I type a few of my problems into the "symptom checker." WebMD often makes me think that my head cold is typhoid. There have been several times that I've run across the worst case scenario in that little online feature...like the time I thought I had kidney stones.

I woke up one morning with this pain in my side, right below my rib cage. It really didn't matter which way I turned or positioned myself, the pain was pretty constant and moderately irritating. After nearly two whole days of living with this annoyance, I did what any internet-educated individual would do in my position—I went to WebMD, listed my symptoms, and briefly waited to see the list of my potential medical diagnoses. At the top of the pile, there it was: "kidney stones." I freaked.

After Googling my medical discovery, I quickly learned that passing a kidney stone was the male pain equivalent to giving birth. The stone passed one way and one way only, and that was by peeing it out in a long, slow, excruciating process. I freaked again and called to make an appointment with a doctor.

After sheepishly communicating my symptoms to the physician and a hasty look-see process by her on the horribly uncomfortable examination room recliner with the endless roll of disposable butcher paper, she told me that I, in fact, did not have kidney stones, but a small pulled muscle in my lower abdomen. She briskly gave me an unsympathetic look and a prescription for ibuprofen.

This kidney stone paranoia was a reminder that I'm incredibly quick to put my faith in the most negative of all outcomes. I'll believe the worst before I even come close to believing the best in any given situation that might require my faith. Do you sometimes find yourself in the same boat as me?

Prussian orphanage director and missionary George Mueller once said,

"The beginning of anxiety is the end of faith and the beginning of true faith is the end of anxiety."[18]

If I want to be a person of faith, then anxiety, worry, fear, and mistrust need to become a thing of the past for me. Mueller says that anxiety and faith cannot coexist at the same time, so when my initial reaction to any little problem is a belief in the worst, I am not being a man of faith.

This is not the kind of life I want to continually live and it is certainly not the life that God calls us to as His followers. He is asking us to be men and women of faith and to believe that even in the midst of the worst situations, He lovingly reigns over the entire universe with complete sovereignty.

I shouldn't be so quick to believe the worst, and neither should you. Instead, I should position myself as a humble and faithful child of God that believes in His goodness and grace. As I do, my life will inevitably look different to any onlooker wrestling with the same issues. And after that, opportunities naturally arise to speak with others about the God who has changed me to my core and offers me the opportunity to live in peace instead of turmoil.

All that being said, I wonder if that kind of faith can make me believe the best about the person who invented glitter?

My guess would be "no."

15
FALSE CARICATURES

Have you ever been to an amusement park and sat down in a chair to have one of those pseudo-artists draw a cartoon caricature of you? They ask you what you like or what sport you most enjoy, and after about 30 minutes of holding very still with a goofy smile, the end result is this image of a giant head attached to a miniature little body swinging a baseball bat or something. Everyone ends up looking like one of those old cartoon dudes from the Pep-Boys commercials. Maybe the drawing kind of looks like you, but it's not at all a real representation of who you are.

Years ago, historian A. Toynbee said, "Most people don't reject Christianity, but a false caricature of it."[19] Having worked in ministry with college students for quite some time now, I'd agree with that statement.

There are a bunch of methods that I have adopted in order to engage with people about the topic of God and spirituality and many are great at finding out what some individuals actually think about the subject. One of my preferred methods is an interview tool called *QuEST* (Questions Examining Students' Thinking), which does an excellent job of getting at the heart of what people really believe concerning God, Christ, and Christians. One of my favorite questions of the interview asks, "Suppose your best friend comes to you and says that they want to become a Christian but they don't know how...what would you tell them?"

The reason I love this question is because it makes someone communicate what they think the gospel is and how a person can respond to it. I'm not going to lie, though...about 95% of the time, people get it wrong. The default answer that's usually given has a lot to do with religious activity and very little to do with the grace of God through Jesus. In short, people just don't get it.

Sure, a lot of folks can spout off the textbook answer of "accepting Christ," but most of the people I've interviewed have no clue what it actually means to become a Christian. To most, it means adopting a set of rules to live by, then trying your best to keep at it until something else comes along that's more congruent with the lifestyle they want to live. This is the prevalent belief of our current culture.

But doesn't that make you want to change the culture's perspective on what it means to be a follower of Jesus? It does for me. For some reason, something stirs within me when I know that people think Christianity is just another rulebook governed by tradition, churches, guilt, and Fox News.

Not too long ago, I met a guy named Ali who started coming to the church I attend only because his girlfriend wanted him to. I befriended him over time and asked if he wanted to get together sometime to talk more intentionally about life, love, video games, or whatever. He agreed, so a few days later we met at a little table in a bookstore during the afternoon over a scone and a couple of chai tea lattes. How's that for manly?

Ali is nominally Muslim and his family is the same. He was raised here in the States, but still has some relatives in the Middle East. Over the past few years, Ali has made some connections to the Christian church via friends but would still not call himself a Christian.

When we got together, I decided to tread lightly at first, not knowing how he would respond to a full frontal blast of a gospel presentation, so about 40 minutes went by before we even talked about anything serious. Eventually, I felt that the communication climate was warm enough for me to jump in and ask him if he had any questions about Christianity since he had been coming to the church.

As it turns out, he really didn't have many questions, but he surely did have some preconceived notions about the teachings of Christianity. Like many people, Ali believed that the Christian faith wasn't really faith at all—it was religion. He believed that a person had to follow a set of rules and behave according to what the Bible said to do in order to gain acceptance by God. This gave me a great opportunity to share with Ali what the Bible truly teaches about what it means to have a personal relationship with God.

I told him that every other religion says, "Do these things, then you're a (fill in the religious blank)." But Christianity says, "Accept the gift of salvation for free and you're in. Then you will want to respond in action through gratitude for what God has done for you…it's completely the opposite of what you just described."

I literally saw his face change as he began to understand it.

I'm so thankful that I was able to meet with him and accurately explain what it means to be a true follower of Christ. I believe that Ali no longer has a false caricature of what a Christian is or what we believe and I'm hopeful that, one day, he will place his full trust in Jesus to pay for his sins. I'm not sure what God has in store for him, but I'm very glad that I was faithful to speak up and eliminate the wrong image of Christianity that was distorting the truth of the gospel.

This preconceived notion of Christianity, God, or even "religion" can often get in the way of our efforts to actually make a difference in the lives of those who don't know God. It's a very common stumbling block that people trip over before a journey toward Jesus can even get started. We must do all that we can to help others understand the true anti-religion gospel that leads to salvation. To make that happen, we need to be willing to step into their world where they're at instead of expecting them to show up at our doorstep.

Ali was a rare gift that came along and crossed my path under the roof of my church, but you'll find that situations won't often present themselves like that. We've got to go where the people are (just like Ariel from *The Little Mermaid*) and show them that following Jesus is not the same thing as following religion. They will live with a consistent false caricature that can only be shattered by a living/breathing example of the truth—you.

16
IF YOU'RE SAVED AND YOU KNOW IT, CLAP YOUR HANDS!

There is a common Christian joke that goes something like this: "I'm an atheist before I get my coffee in the morning," or "I don't believe in God before 10:00am."

This, of course, implies that it's difficult to believe that there can be a good God who loves me and created the beautiful world around me when all that runs through my head as my alarm clock honks is, "I would rather die than get out of this bed right now."

I am not a morning person. I am a card-carrying member of the Night Owl Club and ascribe all of my anger in the morning to the fact that morning even exists. I genuinely do not have a problem with morning people, though. I really don't. They can go on being chipper and peppy in the morning all they want to. The problem arises, however, when an overzealous morning person tries to make *me* a morning person...and I truly believe that that is the major problem with any and every hard-core morning person out there. They can't help themselves.

A morning person rises when the sun hits their face, breathes deeply, stretches with joy, and audibly proclaims, "Hooray! It's another day and Jesus is alive! I must share this joy with any human being that is relatively close to where I am at this very second!" They rush to the nearest person resting comfortably in their bed, they jump up onto the base of the mattress where that nearest person is comfortably sleeping and they bounce up and down shouting something completely obnoxious like, "Wake-y, wake-y! Eggs and Bake-y!" Ugh.

Now, many things go through my mind when a morning person makes the sad attempt to convert me to their side (for illustrative purposes, we'll call this side "The Dark Side"). Phrases like "shut up" and "calm down" really don't fully describe the kind of language going through my mind during these occurrences, so I'll just go ahead and quote a few movie lines that might better portray the smattering of thoughts that bubble to the surface in those moments:

1. "In Hong Kong, you'd be dead." –Jet Li, *Lethal Weapon 4*
2. "Should we or should we not follow the advice of the galactically stupid?!" –Tom Cruise, *A Few Good Men*
3. "Take your stinkin' paws off me, you d@m^ dirty ape." – Charlton Heston, *Planet of the Apes*
4. "You'll be sorry, Pee Wee Herman!" –The guy who played Francis, *Pee Wee's Big Adventure*

You get my point. I simply don't want to turn to The Dark Side and I don't believe I ever will. During that time of the day, anything and everything that they say ends up being this annoying attempt to transform me into someone I don't want to be...namely, someone like them.

Is it possible that this is how non-Christians sometimes perceive us and our efforts to "convert" them? A Christian with unbridled zeal for Jesus is an admirable one, but without the proper discernment on how to appropriately communicate the gospel, everyone just ends up with a strong desire to punch that Christian in the face.

I am reminded here of the praise and worship song entitled *Undignified*. I don't doubt that the heart behind this song is pure (probably referencing either 1 Corinthians 4:10 or 2 Samuel 6:22), but with the modern chorus of a song that proclaims "I'll become even more undignified than this" (the "this" is referring to dancing, singing and being crazy for God), I begin to wonder if any Christian's message would be taken seriously by Joe Non-Christian especially after the undignified chorus that is followed up with a triumphant "La la la la, Hey!"[20]

Anyway, back to my thought process—does being "a fool for Christ" really mean that I can intentionally act like an idiot for the sake of Christ at the expense of diminishing the very heart of what I represent?

We are fools for Christ, but you are so wise in Christ! We are weak, but you are strong! You are honored, we are dishonored![21]

I don't think the author of 1 Corinthians (the apostle Paul) is talking about being an idiot for Jesus by acting crazy just because I want to act crazy. In fact, if you read that verse within its context, it is actually talking about persecution...nothing in there about dancing for Jesus.

Because of this common undignified persona running rampant amongst Christians everywhere, I'm not surprised that evangelical believers are frequently stereotyped as grotesquely happy and over-the-top morons that belong on the children's show *The Wiggles* instead of legitimate members of society who have something of significance to offer their fellow man.

A morning person cannot change a non-morning person into a morning person by being a nauseating morning person. Similarly, a giddy Christian who lacks discernment and good communication skills cannot stand on a public street corner in New York City singing, "If you're saved and you know it, clap your hands!" and expect a favorable response from anyone. Okay, maybe that's a radical analogy, but hyperbole might be my best tool to utilize here.

A few summers ago, I watched an interesting reality show on NBC called *Last Comic Standing*. Maybe you've heard of it. It's cancelled now, but I enjoyed it when it ran.

Its format was pretty much like any other reality show in that a million people try out, and the group is eventually whittled down to the top twelve. In this case, they're trying out to be a stand up comic. The top twelve are all thrown together in a house, they're given specific comedy challenges, a few of them get promiscuous in the hot tub, America votes, and they get eliminated one-by-one until it's the last comic standing. Clever, huh?

Well, the specific season that I saw happened to include a top twelve participant that was actually a duo who called themselves "God's Pottery." Essentially, the two guys in the duo played out these characters (much like Sacha Baron Cohen played the character Borat) both in the house and on stage that were supposed to be examples of syrupy sweet Christian camp counselors.

What they were doing was interesting for a couple of reasons. Firstly, as far as I could tell from the footage that was actually used on the show, God's Pottery never broke character. They constantly acted out this annoying pair of evangelicals that would always look at the brighter side of life while smiling and waving to rocks, trees, dogs, and parked cars. Not once did I see them talk to another person in a normal tone or even make a sandwich without praising the Lord.

Secondly, their entire comedy act on stage was just an exaggerated example of what they believed a real Christian was. They didn't tell jokes, they didn't have funny stories or banter, and they didn't even wear normal clothes. Their whole shtick was a mockery of the average American believer. After coming on stage and exclaiming to the audience, "Celibacy rocks!" they would sing kid-praise-type songs on the guitar and get the crowd involved by having them clap their hands and high-five their neighbor if they were saved. Needless to say, they were one of the first to be voted out of the top twelve because they were more tiresome than funny.

I find it disheartening that this is what a lot of people out there think Christians are like. God's Pottery was 'funny' enough to make it to the top twelve on this show by living out a ridiculous parody of the American Christ-follower and I didn't see one person object to the false stereotype.

Now, was it unfair of God's Pottery to generalize every Christian into the irritating and happy-go-lucky characters they played while participating on *Last Comic Standing*? Of course it was...but that's not really why I decided to tell you that this happened. I gave you this example to help you understand that most people out there misunderstand.

A lot of individuals believe Christians are bothersome screwballs that happily try to convert everyone in their path, all the while not knowing that they are really just coming across as the pesky pop-up ad that people want to immediately click away from. If you know that this might be how your efforts to connect with others are received, don't you want to change that? I certainly do. But how?

There are probably several missing ingredients in our "changing the false perception" formula. But I'm convinced that the main thing we're lacking is discernment. Let me add a wrinkle to a statement I made earlier—a morning person cannot make a non-morning person a morning person by being a nauseating morning person...***in the morning***.

What we say and how we say it are of utmost importance, but *when* we say it is of equal value. The time to tell your friend that God works for the good of those who love Him is not right after a close relative of theirs has passed away.

Yes, non-Christians can be insensitive when it comes to their views on what they think we are like, but let's not give them more ammunition for that unfair assumption by being insensitive ourselves and trying to shoehorn the gospel into their lives at inappropriate times. Yes, they need Jesus. Yes, they need to place their faith in Him in order to experience real life, unconditional love, and acceptance. And yes, it is extremely important to share the gospel. But when you proclaim the gospel at the wrong time and place, you become the pretentious radio DJ that everyone loathes but who still calls himself "your boy" in his on-air monologues.

When it comes to the listening ears of this generation, *how, when, where,* and *why* we share the good news of Jesus' death and resurrection for our shortcomings is just as important as saying it. Discernment is a quality that a ton of Christians lack, and this must stop if we are going to be effective in communicating the truth that can and will change people's lives.

17
ALL ABOUT YOU?

You need to be dwelling on thoughts like: I am creative. I am talented. I have a bright future. My best days are still out in front of me.
JOEL OSTEEN

I really like thinking about how great of a guy I am. I know that sounds bad, but regrettably, it's true.

I'm a genius when it comes to the subject of me. I'm literally obsessed with myself. Not a day goes by when I don't think, "What could make me happier right now?" or "What do I want to do?" And if you were honest, you'd probably say the same thing about yourself. Am I right?

Self-obsession has always been a human problem, but recently I think we've taken it to new levels. Ask any kid what they want to be when they grow up and this is what they'll most likely tell you: a rock star, an actor, a fashion designer, or a superstar athlete. Hop in a time machine and ask the same question to a kid 20 years ago, and you'd get a very different answer with a very different mindset: a fireman, a mom, a police officer, or an army soldier. Yesteryear used to be about giving of yourself to make the world a better place. Now it's about how to achieve the most success and get the most money to live in a big house with fancy cars and cool clothes while basking in the light of your own fame. I know I'm probably sounding a bit like a crotchety old man here, complaining about the present or longing for the past, but more and more I keep seeing what a "me-centered" society is doing to our thought process and belief system…and it isn't good.

Of course culture is going to continue to get worse. This doesn't shock me at all. What does bother me, however, is when we allow the tainted teaching of the culture around us to shape our views of the church, the body of believers within it, and God Himself.

I'll let you in on a not-so-big secret from the bible: it's not about you—it's about Jesus Christ!

People like Dr. Phil, Tony Robbins, and Joel Osteen want *you* to believe that if *you* work hard enough to become a better *you* and believe that the capability is inside of *you* to achieve the greatness that *you* deserve, *you* will aspire to great things. The only small, little, tiny problem is this: you're simply not capable of being better in your own power.

Whoops...that kind of changes everything, doesn't it?

No matter how hard I try, I have never, ever been able to make my sinful nature improve by trying harder to become a better me. Every seven-step program that I have implemented into my daily routine has failed miserably. All the sincere promises I have made to God or myself to "try harder" and "do better the next time" have come up wanting in the end. In my own power, I am a loser ten times out of ten. Why? Because I can't do it on my own! I need Jesus!

And so do you.

It's a warm and fuzzy feeling when someone tells you that you are capable of achieving prominence. But what does that desire for prominence ultimately produce? Most often, the goal of self-improvement is self-glorification. See, when you peel back the warm and fuzzy layers of self-esteem, there is a dark and disgusting idol that rests in the center of the shiny exterior—pride.

Nobody today likes to admit that they need help. We all fantasize about sitting in the chair opposite of Oprah Winfrey while being applauded by the studio audience for pulling ourselves up by our bootstraps and making it on our own (well, at least I fantasize about that).[22]

"Nobody helped me on my way to the top."

"I did it all by myself."

"I worked hard and I achieved my goals."

"I believed in my heart that I could do it and I did."

Often revered as the American ethic of "individualism," these are the kind of statements the culture admires and praises. These are the phrases that make people tear up and silently proclaim, "Good for them!" And unfortunately, this is the prevailing mentality that has oozed its way into the church, bringing with it the destructive arrogance that has been the downfall of humanity time and time again.

In Genesis 11, all the people at the Tower of Babel thought very highly of themselves and consequently, the Lord intervened to help them understand their rightful place, in terms of importance. He confused their speech so that they literally couldn't understand one another, and their plan to make a name for themselves had a giant God-shaped monkey wrench thrown into it.

Now, please understand what I'm saying here and what I'm not. I'm not saying that you are worthless garbage. I'm not saying that you aren't valuable and special either. You are very important to God...if you weren't, do you think He would have sent His only Son, Jesus Christ, to die for you? You have incredible worth *because* of what God has done for you through Jesus Christ as His image-bearer.

The problem begins to take shape, however, when we get cocky and think that all of life is about us and what we can do to make a name for ourselves (like the folks in Genesis 11). God is very clear about the fact that He will not share His glory with anyone. He is jealous for it and when we try to steal His glory for ourselves, it is sin...even if it's masked by the perpetual back-patting happiness of self-esteem motivators.

All of you, clothe yourselves with humility toward one another, because, "God opposes the proud but gives grace to the humble."
I PETER 5:5

A good definition of humility is "knowing your place." God is God and we are not. The quicker we realize this, the better off we will be, I promise.

Success in life doesn't come by believing in the capability we have to be better people; it comes by knowing our place and believing that God is the ultimate benevolent power and loving authority over all things, including our lives.

But if we swallow the world's idea of self-esteem, we are essentially worshipping ourselves and making our own glorification the end-all-be-all of life on earth. Although it may seem natural to revel in the idea of self-glory because it feels great, that kind of existence is dangerous living to any believer that follows Christ. You cannot have two people sitting on the throne of your life. Either God will be calling the shots, or you will.

It may seem a bit scary to give control over to Him when everything sinful inside of you screams for the opposite, but true freedom only comes from handing your life over to God and trusting that He'll do the best job while sitting in the driver's seat. Jesus laid His life down for us, so now we can be quick to yield our own lives to Him. He deserves our complete surrender.

18
YOUR JAPANESE HERO, BABY

Growing up as an Air Force kid (or "brat" as we are commonly known) gives a child many unique experiences that normal kids never get to go through. For example, when I was a boy of about 9 or 10, my family and I got to visit Tokyo Disneyland. The atmosphere there was much like what you might think it would be (a carbon copy of the American Disneyland), but the one major difference was that *we* were the minority as a white family from California.

Nearly everything around us was completely recognizable because of the familiar Disney branding, but all of the "cast members" (a.k.a. employees) were Japanese and spoke in their native tongue. Consequently, when Cinderella or Prince Charming approached us, we had no clue what they were saying. My minority status became all the more real to me when I was specifically chosen out of a line waiting to see the interactive *Fantasia* theater experience.

An adorable Japanese woman in uniform approached me and made a request in Japanese. She clearly wanted me to volunteer to be a part of something in the show, but because of the language barrier, none of us understood exactly what I was being asked to do.

To my horror, both of my folks said something like, "Sure, take him!" and I found myself being led away from the crowd and into a secluded part of the building where I was sure that I was going to become the next victim in a long line of American children kidnapped while ignorantly enjoying the pleasures of a Disney-themed amusement park in Tokyo.

The next few moments were kind of hazy (perhaps they drugged me), but from what I recall, I found myself standing on a small platform in front of the woman in uniform and holding a giant glowing plastic sword in both of my little hands. The platform started to lift itself upward, and I looked around in amazement as I slowly ascended into the middle of a coliseum-type theater, surrounded by what seemed like 10,000 delighted Japanese guests.

I was blown away. I had never seen this many people in my entire life, and they were all there looking at me! I quickly noticed that nearly everyone was taking pictures and pointing to the area that was directly opposite of where I was standing with the young woman. I looked in the direction that they were pointing and what I saw next would make any kid my age pee their pants in trepidation.

Staring right at me with his glowing evil eyes was the giant demon-like creature from the *Fantasia* movie. He was flanked by two giant puffs of smoke pouring out from the fake volcano behind him. His huge mouth roared with anger and I immediately froze with dread.

The woman behind me said a bunch of things to me that I couldn't understand, so I just turned around and looked at her with a sense of hope that she would save me from the clutches of this vile creature that would surely drag me down into the depths of hell...after he seared my flesh with fire, of course. She said a few more things in Japanese and I shrugged and yelled, "I don't know what you're saying!"

She then grabbed both of my shoulders, turned me around to face the monster, placed her hands over mine as I held the sword, and helped me point it right at the creature. She spouted off a few more words in Japanese and made some weird gun noises with her mouth as we aimed the sword at the monster's face. The demon then recoiled in defeat because of my heroic and noble efforts as the savior of everyone present. The theater erupted with applause (and a lot more incomprehensible words) and all was well with the world again.

After it was all over, my uniformed sidekick placed a medal around my neck and said a few more things to me that I could not decipher. I smiled when my parents eventually came to find me, and I glowed with pride because of my victory over evil. To this day, I still have that little medal stashed away in a trunk.

I remember the feeling I had when I couldn't figure out what was being communicated as I was being shepherded away from my folks and asked to stand on a dark platform while holding a sword. I remember the confusion I encountered when the uniformed woman was telling me to do something rather important as the Prince of Darkness was staring me down in the middle of the theater that day. Even though it ended well for me (clearly my victory was not at all scripted), I was bewildered and scared because I wasn't aware of what was going on.

The point I'm trying to make is this: when you communicate in a language that your intended receiver does not understand, you're doing that person a disservice because you will make zero progress in your attempt to connect and clearly interact. The uniformed woman couldn't help it because she didn't speak English. But if two people are verbally missing each other in their attempts to connect, enlightenment will not come and frustration will abound.

Have you ever tried to make someone understand what you were saying when they didn't speak your language? You start doing all kinds of crazy things to get your message across. Yelling and grandiose hand motions generally take over pretty quickly and you usually end up looking like a complete fool.

Believe it or not, we do this *all the time* as Christians. Maybe not with the hand motions or yelling, but we certainly have a tendency to speak in a language that others don't understand. I'm talking about the dialect we use called *Christianese*.

Christianese are words or phrases that makes sense when

you're inside the Christian subculture, but are completely foreign anywhere else outside of that context. Here are some examples of what I'm talking about:

- Walk with God (As in "How's your walk with God?")
- Quiet time
- Serve the Lord
- Saved
- Fellowship
- Begotten (I once heard a street preacher quote from the King James Version saying, "God sent His only begotten Son!" Confused looks from the crowd were in abundance.)
- Reconciled
- Sanctification
- Thought-life
- Sin (Surprisingly enough, I've run into a ton of people that really don't understand what the term "sin" means.)
- Holy
- Perichoresis (OK, you probably don't use that one very much.)

I could go on and on, but I think you get the picture. Maybe some of these are extreme examples for you and you're thinking that you'd never use words like these in front of non-Christians. If so, great! But you'd be surprised how often we tend to speak *Christianese* when talking about God with others.

To connect with others in the world and really bring clarity to the message of what we believe means being intentional about speaking a language that normal people can understand. And when I say "normal," I mean people who have never darkened the doorway of a church, never opened a Bible, never bothered to pray much, and never tried to watch *The Passion of the Christ*.

It's so important that we are consciously thinking about what *they* would understand when we describe our faith in Jesus. Using *Christianese* is confusing and somewhat ridiculous when we're trying to relate with people who need to know about Him. That's why it is vital that we break down any walls previously built by the Christian community that might be a barricade to someone understanding the truth. If we are deliberate about this, it opens up more avenues for clarity of the message.

The apostle Paul was a master at this. He was always very intentional about using the kind of language that people would be able to understand, depending on his specific environment. Sometimes, he would literally speak the language that his listeners would understand best. For example:

When they heard him speak to them in Aramaic, they became very quiet.
ACTS 22:2

In this section of the book of Acts, Paul uses the Aramaic language to connect with his audience so that they would best understand the message of the gospel. And if you read on in the chapter, he begins his presentation with a sort-of verbal Jewish resume in order to connect even better.

Now, this doesn't really seem like rocket science when we hear about it. We think to ourselves, "Of course he spoke their language. It wouldn't make any sense not to." And this is completely my point.

Christianese is a language that we assume people understand wherever we go, but in truth, it might be as foreign to them as Portuguese (if they're not from Brazil). If we are sensitive to this fact, we will intentionally use the proper words and phrases that best represent our faith without inducing confusion. Notice that in the second part of Acts 22:2, "they became very quiet." Why? Because people listen when they comprehend something interesting. And the gospel in all of its glorious wonder is extremely interesting.

To build obstacles for others on the road to comprehension is a tragedy on our part, and I believe using Christianese does that very thing. I understood this all too well during my demon-slaying adventure in Tokyo that day. It's so very important to identify Christianese in your everyday use, and purge it from your tongue. Clarity, not ignorance, is bliss.

19
REALITY ALTERING PERCEPTIONS

Almost every time I refer to my dad, I am talking about my stepdad, Dave. My mom and my father got divorced when I was three years old, and my mom remarried when I was six. Since that time, my dad (step dad, Dave...stay with me here) raised me as his own son. He taught me how to golf, how to drive, how to have appropriate table manners, and made fun of me when I liked certain girls from school. He paid for me to go to college and showed me what it meant to be a man that appropriately respects authority. I love my dad dearly and continually try to communicate that to him whenever I get the chance.

My biological father is a horse of a different color. Although he tried to show his care and appreciation for me as his son early on in my youth, I believe he quickly became bored with the idea of being a father and really had a greater desire to be an impressive icon that my sister and I would worship. Consequently, my father was prone to stretching the truth when it came to tales about himself or achievements he had made both in the financial realm or physical altercations with idiotic obstacles that chose to stand in his way, even when warned to step aside. More accurately, he was a liar and unfortunately still is to this day.

However, as a 10 year-old boy, you'll believe pretty much anything that an adult relative tells you because there is really no reason to question what they say...especially if that relative is your own father. So naturally, I believed him when he said that he had once played for the Tampa Bay Buccaneers. I believed him when he told me that, when his new business contract came through, he would have enough money to buy me any car I wanted as soon as

I turned sixteen. Children are innocent suckers that can be easily hypnotized by delusions of grandeur, spilling from the lips of a father, and I was surely one of them.

But something happened that year when I was ten. Something that would open my eyes to my father's lies and turn my face to the truth that hid behind the walls of deception he had built around me since the time of my parent's separation.

From the time of my mom's remarriage, she had legal custody of my sister and me, and my natural father had summer visitation rights that lasted for about eight weeks or so while school was out each year. In the summer of 1987, my dad (step dad, Dave) was stationed at an Air Force base on the island of Guam, so when it came time to switch parents for a couple of months, flying back to the States wasn't a quick little jaunt across town…it was basically a trip around the world.

Summertime meant no school and that fact alone can vividly color the experiences of a grade-schooler, drastically upping the "fun quotient" of most any occurrence in a kid's life. Playing all day, eating whatever we wanted, and watching any movie we desired were par for the course when it came to the summer visitation ritual. And we soaked it up and savored it like a sugar ant on a discarded lollipop.

My natural father knew this and cleverly rode that enjoyment wave all the way to week eight of our time together, whereby he casually suggested that my sister and I should live with him for the upcoming school year and not return to Guam where my "mean mom" would make us follow all the strict rules. Of course, he had no legal leg to stand on, but the key to his success was convincing his children that their mom was the bad one and that she really didn't want us anyway.

Our little ears became filled with his lies: That our mother spent his child support checks on shoes and the only real reason that she wanted custody of us was for the money. That she didn't actually care about us or love us the way that he did. And that, if we wanted to stay with him, his door would always be open.

Now, in actuality, all evidence was to the contrary of his words… but again, the judgment of a child can be easily manipulated when the communicator appears to have your best interest in mind. And like any gullible young person, my sister and I both bought it. We immediately told him that we did, in fact, want to stay with him and not return to my mom for the coming school year. So, instead of putting us on the appropriate plane to return us to our mom at the end of the summer, my father took us on a mind-numbing trip to an amusement park that would reinforce our belief that we had made the right decision to stay with the "fun parent."

Naturally, my mom freaked out when we didn't show up in the airport at the allotted time, and she frantically made call after call to find out where her children were and why they hadn't come home. Chaos developed for her in the coming days, and through many tears and anxiety-induced nausea, my mom was ready to throw in the towel and succumb to our childhood wishes of staying with our father forever. Only after the stern prompting of a military base chaplain there in Guam did my mom change her mind.

"If you don't fight for your children now, you will regret it for the rest of your life," he said. So my mom fought.

Legally, the power was on her side, and I'll never forget that night when a lawyer and two uniformed police officers showed up at my father's house to take my sister and me away. As we were driven away in the lawyer's car, I was fully convinced that the bad guys were winning and that my mom, in her anger for our defiance, would surely punish us severely once we got back.

We cried nearly the whole flight back to Guam. My father had convinced me that my mother didn't really love or want me, and the only reason she was doing this was to rub it in his face that she was the powerful one. Things were going to be horrible when I got back; I just knew it.

When the plane landed in Guam, I remember looking at my sister through tears. I was so afraid that as soon as my mom saw us, she would grab us by the arm and say with a scowl, "How could you do this? You are such bad children!"

But that's not what happened at all.

After we got off the plane and walked through the terminal, my mom spotted us from across the room and *ran* to greet us—flashing not a scowl, but a wide smile. She embraced both of us at the same time and exclaimed, "I'm so happy that you're home! I missed you so much!" She kissed us and picked us up. My step dad playfully poked me in the stomach and while tapping me on the back said, "Glad to see you back!" (By far his most used and corny joke.)

In that moment, I remember being so thrilled that they were acting the way they were, but at the same time, so confused by my clearly false expectations of what this reunion would look like. Only after a long talk on the living room floor at home did I begin to understand the perspective that I simply could not see before. Lies were exposed, truths were revealed, and the view I had of my natural father was never the same again.

I tell you this story for the specific purpose of illustrating the kind of trap we can fall into if we allow ourselves to be deceived by the Evil One, Satan. No, I'm not subtly trying to tell you that my natural father is exactly like the Devil. What I am trying to do is draw you a picture so you can clearly understand the complexities of unearthing the truth when you are exposed to a series of very believable lies.

See, my father convinced me that my mother did not really want me. She had custody over us for the money. She was never a fun and a strict enforcer of many ridiculous rules. She was short tempered and works-based when it came to her acceptance of my sister and me. I shouldn't want to be with her when I could have fun and do whatever I wanted with my "fun parent," who *really* loved me.

My father whispered these lies into my head all summer long and those lies twisted my perception of reality. Only when I was confronted face to smiling face with the truth did I discover what was really going on. I then became keenly aware of how my mother felt. She wanted what was best for me. She fought for me. She embraced me. She missed me. She loved me.

There are so many parallels to our relationship with God here that I don't really even know where to begin, so instead of trying to hash them all out for you, I'll just say this: God is madly in love with humanity, but Satan doesn't want you to believe that.

If you are a distracted Christian, you are a Christian without impact. If your concentration is focused on questions about God's love for you, will you really be able to wholeheartedly influence others as a joyful slave set free by His love? No...and that is exactly what the Evil One wants.

Satan knows that if he can whisper lies into Christian ears and cause spiritual paralysis, those very believers will pose no serious threat to him. Distraction is a clever and strategic method he employs to render us useless in Kingdom work. But simply knowing this can better equip you for living a life *in* the world but not *of* it. In the grand scheme of things, we are all as gullible as 10 year-old children. If, however, we focus our little eyes on the fact that God is madly in love with us, our tendencies to be drawn off course by the lies of Satan will surely diminish.

I learned some very hard life lessons at an early age, which, dibly painful, clarified my perception of truth and ent run-ins with some very tall tales. As a result, my life bred wisdom and discernment—two gifts ...nually thank God.

God is in love with you. He cherishes you. He died to be with you. Meditate on this and the whispering lies of the Evil One will not alter your perception of reality one bit.

The thief comes only to steal and kill and destroy. I came that they may have life and have it abundantly. I am the good shepherd. The good shepherd lays down his life for the sheep.

JOHN 10:10-11, ESV

20
THE SLOW CREEP

When it comes to the personal preference of most any American, faster is better. I want what I want and I want it right now. Instant gratification is now the norm and the act of waiting for anything is a complete outrage. If things aren't done expeditiously, the annoyance of waiting is simply unbearable.

For example, whenever I have to wait in line at the grocery store, my mind instantly starts to complain about how lame the place is and how, if they really cared about their customers, they'd open up more checkout lanes. As I stand there behind my cart, I silently whine, "Come on, people! My mint chocolate-chip ice cream is going to melt soon and if I don't get home in the next few minutes, I'm going to miss the beginning of *Ultimate Air Jaws* on the Discovery Channel! How hard is it to open up one more flippin' line?"

And trust me, I'm not the only one who hates it when people (as my Mom puts it) "dilly-dally." The "patience is a virtue" cliché hasn't really soaked into the fabric of American society, and I don't think it ever will. Even the quote at the front end of *Talladega Nights: The Ballad of Ricky Bobby* proves my point.

*America is all about speed. Hot, nasty, bad-*** speed.*
ELEANOR ROOSEVELT, 1936

Immediacy is the name of the game, and it's everywhere around us: blazing fast Internet speeds, overnight FedEx delivery, laser hair removal, Hot Pockets, and the like. If you can't get it quick, it pretty much isn't worth getting at all.

I guess this is why the things that move slowly in this world stand in such graphic contrast to the pace of the surrounding environment. Things like a hand-written letter are a rarity when someone opens up their mailbox nowadays and I'm personally taken by surprise when I'm blessed enough to get one. Moreover, if a meal takes longer than thirty minutes to prepare, my wife often skips that recipe when she is flipping through a cookbook. See what I mean?

And since time-occupying things like this are so uncommon in the modern world we live in, they often have an effect on us that we are unable to ignore. Case in point: Thanksgiving dinner is always worth talking about because it usually takes all day to prepare. Or gloating about finishing a 1000-page novel becomes unavoidably commonplace because it probably takes triple the time to read in comparison to a normal book. In short, the more time, the more noteworthy and influential.

Those who are savvy know this.

A friend of a friend of mine started up a restaurant in Orlando, Florida (the chain-restaurant capital of the world), specializing in slow-cooked pork barbeque. He goes to pain-staking lengths to make sure that the food he serves is quality meat, cooked slowly over an absurd amount of time. Why? Because when it's cooked slower, it tastes better. And his deliberate actions in barbeque preparation have paid off in spades. Every day, there is a line out the door from when they open to when they close. People are willing to wait in line for that slow-cooked pork barbeque in 98 degree weather with 100% humidity because they know that they are getting a quality-made tasty product.

Unfortunately, our enemy, the Evil One, has also adopted this slow-moving strategy when it comes to influencing humanity to walk toward the direction that leads to destruction. Let me explain what I mean by that…

Somebody once told me that if I were confronted with the

opportunity to commit an egregious sin right now, I probably wouldn't. However, if the idea of that sin were steadily fed to me over a long period of time, bit-by-bit, I'd be more likely to give in and succumb to the temptation of that sin because of the nature by which it was presented—the slow creep. He was right when he said this because it happens to people *all the time*.

Sadly, our culture is full of examples of individuals who have claimed loyalty to Christ, yet over time, have taken the all-too-familiar face-plant from grace in the public eye. I could probably go on and on about who did what over a certain period of time, but that simply isn't crucial to my overarching point. The truth is that it's extremely easy to point fingers at the countless number of people who have royally screwed up and should have been a better example for Jesus, but quite frankly, apart from the grace of God Almighty, you and I would be in the exact same place as the ones who have failed.

At the end of every episode of the 1980's cartoon series, *G.I. Joe*, there was a kind of "public service announcement" for the kids watching. It could be anything from eating right to refraining from swimming in a pond when a lightning storm is coming. The cool thing was that at the end of each quick lesson, one of the characters from the show would always end the program by saying, "Knowing is half the battle." This statement is particularly true when it comes to the slow creep.

If you are completely unaware of the fact that you are slowly being attacked by an Enemy who is looking to utterly destroy you, the odds of a continued thriving walk with God are not at all in your favor. However, if you are cognizant of the Evil One and the tools he uses to slowly chip away at your passion for godly living, you will know how to appropriately defend yourself from his persistent assaults. Everyone has "chinks in their armor," so to speak. We all have weaknesses. But if we're aware that our Enemy knows the nature and location of those weaknesses, we can set ourselves up for triumph by shielding ourselves from Satan's attacks on our soft spots.[23]

When you trusted in Christ to pay the penalty for your sins and began following Him, you became a serious threat to the Evil One. You essentially painted a big red spiritual target on your chest. I'm not going to lie—Satan has a lot of ammunition to fire at that target in order to take you out of the game, so you'll end up as just another example of someone who let the slow creep gradually devour them. I shudder when I think about the possibility of that happening to me, but all I can do is choose to walk by faith today and pray for the continued grace of God to direct and empower me as I travel the route that leads me on into the future. The same goes for you.

So now you know. And knowing is half the battle.

21
YER MOMMA!

I'd rather pick flowers instead of fights.
OWL CITY

Back in grade school, I would avoid confrontation like the plague. Wait, what am I saying? I *still* avoid confrontation like the plague. I hate it.

Fighting with other people isn't something that I ever willingly step into because, most of the time, I usually end up resorting to childish insults like "Shut up, stupid!" or "Yer momma!" when I'm in the heat of a verbal battle. Cleverly worded retorts don't necessarily rise to the top for me when I'm angry and later on, I almost always regret what has come out of my mouth. Consequently, I have to do a lot of apologizing in subsequent conversations because I've said something that crosses the line.

Recently, I've noticed that many people in my life are also non-confrontational like me. They recoil at the very thought of making a scene or disturbing the peace. Even when someone has a blatant disregard for propriety in front of children or senior citizens, they'd rather stay quiet than ruffle any feathers.

Now, although I am similar, I can't say that I'm exactly the same way because if someone crosses the line in front of Grandma, I'll probably put them in their place regardless of the setting. However, with all that being said, I always prefer harmony over dissonance. And I believe that most American Christians would probably check that box if given the choice.

We desperately don't want to offend people because we really like being liked…and this is where the offensiveness of the gospel creates a major rub in the hearts of non-confrontational believers.

I may be non-confrontational in a large part of my being, but I'm straight shooter. Thus, I like to challenge myself by finding pieces of Scripture that simply make me feel uncomfortable. Here's an example of a verse you can't really hide from:

> *How can you believe if you accept praise from one another, yet make no effort to obtain the praise that comes from the only God?*
>
> JOHN 5:44

This just might be the verse that perfectly describes the condition of all humanity. The approval of others is like a drug and all of us are addicted. We can't get enough of looking our best in the eyes of everyone around us, so if something comes along to threaten that, our natural inclination is to flee. And in the name of Christians being "non-confrontational," most of our culture is going unreached for Jesus Christ.

Sure, we think most Americans have a basic understanding of what the bible teaches about salvation and what it means to be a Christian, but the truth is that they really don't have a clue. It's getting to the point now that when someone tells me that they've gone to church all of their life, I won't even assume that they have a clear definition of the word *sin*. Our assumption that people already understand how to have a relationship with God is foolish. And this drastic error will deteriorate the church from the inside.

Confrontation with others is inevitable. It's got to happen if we are going to make sure that (a) the gospel gets shared and (b) the right kind of people are growing into the right kind of leaders within our church families and ministries. There's really no way around it.

Sometimes part of me just wants to yell at myself and say, "Suck it up, loser" and press forward, but I doubt that anyone would be inspired by that kind of language (myself included). Dealing with the fear of confrontation probably lies more in facing our love for the praise of men more than the praise from God (John 5:44, 12:43). Here, we really start to get at the root of the true problem. Loving the praise of people is very much an idol that replaces the love we have *for* God and want *from* God. By recognizing that this stumbling block exists in our hearts, we are one step closer to digging it out so that we can begin to heal.

I know that it's a cliché, but God's opinion is really the only opinion that matters, and the sooner we realize this and live our life accordingly, the more fulfilled, content, and effective we will be as followers of Christ. People are fickle, and the constant effort it takes to please them is as tiresome as keeping up with a candy obsessed five year-old on Halloween. Why should we live our life for the benefit of others' approval when we know that God accepts us completely in His Son? There is no need to perform for Him! A firm grasp of that truth would be revolutionary for many praise-seeking American Christians if only they could stop thinking about what others thought of them long enough to accept the truth.

This perspective changed my thought pattern and day-to-day behavior once I was finally able to believe that God was totally thrilled with me. The opinions of others became less and less of an obstacle, and I consequently became more and more effective in my faith.[24]

Now when I'm in a confrontation that gets too heated, I'm able to ignore someone's judgmental comments and never think twice when I retort confidently with, "Yer Momma!" That last sentence was a joke…kind of.

PART THREE

THINGS TO MOTIVATE YOU

INTRODUCTION: WHAT'S THE POINT?

Now that you are a bit more aware of what exactly "the world" is and what obstacles can stop you from moving forward, let us move on to the age-old question, "What's the point?"

Why should a follower of Jesus Christ (someone professing the Christian faith) want to genuinely be in the world but not of it? What would motivate me to live like that when I'm far more comfortable in my nice, safe, American evangelical environment?

Well, ignorance really can be bliss when you live in a Christian bubble that blinds you from the reality that people are dying without knowing God. The Christian bubble can truly be a happy place for most believers because it's a small taste of what we think life should be like all the time:

1. I'm surrounded by people who share my beliefs about the most important things in life.
2. I can be vulnerable here and show my true colors.
3. I'm encouraged to draw closer to God as I walk with Him.
4. Others are keeping me accountable in that walk with God.
5. There is a vast pool of dating options if I happen to be single.

And so on, and so on…

Yes, that environment has some benefits (accountability, potential spouse) and it does let us experience a little sampling of heaven (worship, fellowship, etc). However, I believe that there are a variety of reasons to frequently emerge from the Christian bubble, and I'm going to attempt to explore as many of them as I can.

Before you take the first step on a journey, you have to know why it's important to take that journey in the first place. In the words of the proverbial over-dramatic actor, "What's my motivation?" Like most pursuits in life, we should know the "Why" before we know the "How."

So, the correct answer to the question, "What's the point?" is, "Well, there's a lot of them." And therein lies the challenge.

If I can help you to recognize the fact that there are many reasons why you should live your life in the world but not of the world, perhaps you will become antsy with the thought that too much of your life is being spent surrounded by Christians. Maybe you will begin to see that God wants to use you in a way that you've never been used before, and the thought of that happening makes you giddy like a kid on Christmas Eve. Okay, maybe not giddy, but excited.

Fear of the awkward might be your greatest obstacle here, but jumping over that obstacle will prove to be very rewarding. On your mark, get set...

22
ARE YOU READY FOR SOME SOFTBALL?

A few years ago, I went to see an intramural softball game with my father-in-law, Ed. My wife's brother was playing in the game that consisted mostly of people from my in-laws' church. Don't let that fool you, though; a lot of these church dudes could absolutely crush a softball out into the parking lot without even thinking about it. None of the minivans parked just beyond the outfield were safe.

We got to the game about five minutes before it was supposed to start, leaving us enough time to pick a good viewing spot. We busted out our lawn chairs and waited for things to get rolling.

The players on both teams were practicing their throws and swings when I noticed a glaring absence from the field—the umpire. Game time had arrived and nobody was actually there to call the game. I overheard a random discussion from some of the players about what I had just noticed, and looks of concern began to spread pretty quickly over everyone's faces. Nobody wanted to forfeit the game, but they needed an umpire there to make sure that the score could be accurately recorded in order to have the game catalogued in the system for appropriate rankings and what not. I know, I know…this all seemed a bit much for me too, but church softball leagues have a tendency to take themselves very seriously and I wasn't about to openly mock the system while a bunch of large, angry softball players were close enough to swing a metal bat at my face.

Everyone waited for another ten minutes or so and the two team captains shuffled over to each other and had a little talk. All of us sitting in our lawn chairs quickly learned what they were discussing when one of them turned toward us and shouted to the crowd, "Does anyone here want to call the game for us?"

My father-in-law knows the game of baseball pretty well, so I wasn't really all that surprised when he quickly responded to the open request with, "I'll do it!" Ed then rose from his lawn chair, casually walked over behind home plate, and began to call balls and strikes as the game got underway.

I'll never forget that moment because as I watched him umpire the game, I remembered thinking, "Hmm...Ed has gone from a casual spectator of this softball game to being very much involved in its outcome."

You know, the kind of experience that Ed went through happened a lot in the bible, too. No, I'm not talking about softball games and lawn chairs[25], but I am referring to making the move from being a casual spectator to active participant. Here's an example from Mark 4:35-41:

That day when evening came, he said to his disciples, "Let us go over to the other side." Leaving the crowd behind, they took him along, just as he was, in the boat. There were also other boats with him. A furious squall came up, and the waves broke over the boat, so that it was nearly swamped. Jesus was in the stern, sleeping on a cushion. The disciples woke him and said to him, "Teacher, don't you care if we drown?" He got up, rebuked the wind and said to the waves, "Quiet! Be still!" Then the wind died down and it was completely calm. He said to his disciples, "Why are you so afraid? Do you still have no faith?" They were terrified and asked each other, "Who is this? Even the wind and the waves obey him!"

Up until this time, the disciples had really just been observers of what Jesus was doing in His ministry on earth. Now, at the prompting of their leader, they've gotten in a boat and been lead directly into a storm they didn't ask for. Their faith is tested by the crazy events in nature, and unfortunately for them, they have come up wanting in the Belief Department.

I have a tendency to scoff at the disciples when I read stories like this and murmur to myself, "Yeah, you punks. Where *is* your faith? Jesus has been revealing Himself to you and you still don't believe yet?" But as my grandma used to say, "When you point one finger at someone, you've got four other fingers pointing right back at yourself." Now, of course that's not true at all, because when I point at something, there is no possible way to have all my other regular fingers pointing back at me while my thumb does the same thing. My hand is not a misshapen claw whose opposable thumb twists awkwardly to extend itself in the same direction as my other fingers when I make a fist.

Oh, grandma…she may have her understanding of the human anatomy all messed up, but principally she's correct. I'm always quick to point out the flaws of the disciples, but in my heart I know that I would have been the exact same way if I were in their sandals.

We are all faced with spiritual moments in life that take us from casual spectators to active participants; especially when it comes to being a person of faith. Yes, we had faith to accept the payment for the penalty of our sins when we became Christians, but do we have that same day-to-day, moving-out-of-our-comfort-zone, trusting-God-no-matter-what kind of faith? Probably not.

Walking by faith is something that we talk a lot about in Christian circles. The problem, however, is that we just don't do it very much. When faced with a specific challenge to be actively involved in the world but not of the world, it is going to take active faith. And that can be extremely difficult and awkward to live out.

It's easy to sit and be a spectator…the chairs are comfortable and we don't feel like we're in danger. But God doesn't want us to live a mundane existence of sitting and watching the world go by. He wants us to participate in the action so badly that He's willing to shake us out of our apathy and lead us into a storm—just like He did with the disciples. It takes faith to do that.

Faith is something that God values in a way that I don't think I will ever comprehend. I may not necessarily understand it completely, but I know that God wants me to live in it and walk by it moment-by-moment. If I do, I get a glimpse of the abundant life Jesus talked about: I can live life to its fullest. I am involved in the game instead of just watching it. I am doing what I was created to do. I am inside the will of my Father God.

Here's hoping that, when God calls us, we all respond with, "I'll do it!" I pray that we all quickly get up from our lawn chairs to walk out behind home plate to be involved in the game. Isaiah 6:8 is a good reminder of what our heart attitude should be:

Then I heard the voice of the Lord saying, "Whom shall I send? And who will go for us? "And I said, "Here am I. Send me!"

23
BILLY ZANE'S PREDICTION

God Himself could not sink this ship.

Billy Zane's infamous foreshadowing no doubt made everyone who saw James Cameron's *Titanic* think, "Ha-ha. He's wrong. What an idiot."

Right around the time that *Titanic* came out in theaters and began to take the world by storm, I wondered what all the hoopla was about. So after a lot of thought and prayerful reflection (sarcastic tone implied), I finally made the decision to add to the billions it was raking in and see the movie that made every woman on earth go to the theater every weekend for a month and cry until they were dehydrated. The critics were right; it was an emotional film. I actually began to feel myself get upset as the credits rolled . . . me, a dude. Can you believe that? What was wrong with me?

A film like this had never moved me, so I did what any man of my maturity level would do. As I exited, I passed the theater of the later screening that was happening right next door, I opened the door to the room and yelled inside, "The boat sinks!" That made me feel better and all was right with the world again.

Sure, *Titanic* is a bit dated now, but the truth of the matter is that the flick made people a bit obsessed with the sunken ship. At the time, everyone was hungry for random facts about the *Titanic* and what happened the night it went down.

For example, here are a few things you might already know about the "Ship of Dreams"...

1. There were 2200 passengers aboard *Titanic.*
2. 700 people survived the sinking of the ship.

3. 20 lifeboats went out from the sinking ship carrying those survivors.
4. Immediately after the *Titanic* sank, 328 people were left swimming in the icy cold water.

I remember that scene in the movie when the ship goes down. The camera pans out and you can see all the people splashing around in the water, freezing and calling out for help. The people swimming in the water know that there are lifeboats floating in the near distance with plenty of room for most of the drowning people. So they yell for help, they yell for rescue, they yell for salvation.

Now, if you've seen the movie, you know that the lifeboats don't paddle over to the swimmers for fear that their boats would be swamped and pulled down as well. They don't want to end up in the water themselves, so they selfishly wait. And they wait. And they wait.

Well, the conscience of one of the lifeboat captains eventually gets the better of him and he commands the boat to go out to look for any remaining survivors in the water. It's been a while, so most of the people in the water have already died, but out of the 328 people in the water at the time of the sinking, six are saved. Only six.

What I realized after I saw this movie was that those 322 people who died in the water that night didn't die because the *Titanic* sank. They died because the people who were already saved didn't turn around and help them.

Interesting spiritual parallel, huh? There are people around us all the time who are crying out for help. Some of them know it, but most of them don't. They're longing to be rescued from the icy grip of sin and God is calling us to turn our lifeboat around to go get them. He wants to use us to make that happen.

Many times in my life, I run across moments when I feel the

tug to open my mouth and speak up about who the Lord is and what He has done to rescue me. These often happen with random people I meet in a restaurant, on a beach, in a store, or around my neighborhood. And unfortunately for me, many times I end up happily waving at those moments as they pass me by because I'm overly concerned that I'm going to make the conversation awkward, thus potentially alienating myself from people I want to impress.

Well, if people truly are in danger without Christ, then those moments I'm afraid to ruin with awkwardness are really more about "life and death" than "me being liked," right? If so, you and I should begin to see the difference and embrace the truth that many are screaming for help. Perhaps we will be quicker to turn our lifeboat around and paddle out into the thick of it all where people need us if we're willing to see reality.

24
GIMME! GIMME! GIMME!

On occasion back when I was in college, my friends and I would go to this home-style restaurant called The Home Place.

The Home Place is the kind of restaurant you think about when one combines the word *Amish* with the word *delectable*...unless you have some kind of a bizarre imagination that takes you in a totally different mental direction (and if that's the case, call your psychiatric health physician immediately).

Anyway, back to the food. Juicy fried chicken, tender roast beef, smoked turkey, mashed potatoes and gravy, green beans, corn on the cob, gravy, biscuits, gravy, cornbread, and iced tea...and gravy. All of this and all you can eat: a dream come true for any college dude looking to work on his freshman fifteen.

The restaurant was a good thirty-minute drive from campus, so more often than not, we'd get up late and go on a weekend for lunchtime. If we knew we were going the next day, sometimes we wouldn't eat dinner that night just so we could justify the gluttony when we got there; that's how good this place was.

The establishment was a converted old farmhouse and the atmosphere inside really added to the home-style country appeal that they were going for. My friends and I all agreed that it was more delicious and more authentic than any of the 6 billion Cracker Barrel restaurants sprinkled throughout the nation. And the size of the line out front of The Home Place always proved us right.

The standard wait time was consistently 30-45 minutes, regardless of when you showed up, and the waiting area was always crowded. It was also torture. When we would put our name in for a table, we would be forced to sit or stand in this little room that I could only assume used to be a small den or mud room back when the place was a functioning house. It was connected to a long hallway that opened up to the main dining area, giving everyone waiting for lunch the perfect view of what it was like to be over-fed and content with the world.

For what would seem like hours, we would loiter in the den with grumbling stomachs and smell all the delicious items as they were piled onto platters and taken to insatiable customers, sitting at crowded tables while demanding from their waitresses, "More chicken! More potatoes! More iced tea! More gravy!" I'm not going to lie: I hated every one of them.

Now, there were basically two types of customers in this restaurant at any given time—the stuffed and the starving. The stuffed were the ones at the tables who continually bellowed for more as they gorged themselves on wonderful home-style cooking. The starving were the poor saps who had to dwell in the waiting room and stare at other people as they ate.

Recently, I heard a talk from someone at a conference that made me come to a shocking realization: the same two types of people exist all over America today—the stuffed and the starving. No, I'm not making a literal commentary on why we should be feeding the poor (which is no doubt very important), but I am talking about the contrast of people in their differing spiritual conditions.

Christians often sit at the table of God and receive His grace, wanting for nothing but more. "It's all about me. How can my church pour into me? What kind of group can I be involved in with believers that will spiritually benefit me? Who will disciple me? What church service has the best preaching? What kind of worship music best caters to my taste? Where can I serve most comfortably but get the most reward? Me, me, me…it's all about me." They are stuffed with the good gifts of God, yet they hold their plates up to

His face and continually shout, "More blessing please!"

The majority of the population, however, is spiritually starving. They have no idea what it truly means to have a personal relationship with God. Whether they realize it or not, they are hungry for the kind of love and blessing that can only come from Jesus Christ, and it's time to pass the plate. If we don't get up from the table and recognize that it isn't always about what spiritually benefits *me* the most, the spiritually starving will continue to grow anemic while we sit and ask for more from God.

As American Christians, we've been given the kind of blessings that are only dreamt about in other parts of the world. There are literally thousands of books that you could go online and buy right this second to help with any type of spiritual issue you might be going through.[26] You can go to any bible-believing church and get plugged in to an environment that feeds and nurtures you in the Lord. There are college and high school ministries all over the nation that pour into Christian students and spur on growth, depth and development as a passionate follower of Jesus. We are spoiled, my friends, and it is time to pass the plate.

Now, am I saying that our spiritual nourishment is a bad thing? Of course not! Each and every follower of Christ needs to connect with a church home that spiritually feeds them and cares for their needs on a regular basis. But if we only stay seated at the table of God and refuse to get up, we are like the overweight people in *Wall*E* who obsess about themselves and continue to do nothing but eat because it's comfortable. Fortunately for lesson's sake, those Disney characters eventually opened their eyes to see the truth… and it's high time we did too.

It's time to pass the plate and stop being "me-centered" Christians who constantly think about only ourselves and what can personally benefit our own spiritual lives. There is danger in constantly saying, "Gimme, gimme, gimme!" to God. We quickly become enamored with only the blessings and not the One who blesses. We single-mindedly focus on what God can do for *me* and when disappointment arises from an unmet expectation, we walk away blaming God that He's never good enough.

In Ephesians 3:2, Paul says, "...God's grace that was given to me for you..."

The Lord's grace was a gift given to Paul for a specific purpose. Sure, it empowered him, but he was also expected to be a good steward of that grace by "spreading the wealth" so to speak. It was given to him for the benefit of others.

If we live as a conduit of God's blessing to others and focus on how to be a servant of His goodness to others in need, we can richly appreciate not only the amazing gifts we receive, but the Giver Himself. And we can't help but speak to anyone we can about how good He truly is.[27]

25
GO TO HELL

If the Christians are right, I'm in trouble.
SETH MACFARLANE, CREATOR OF *FAMILY GUY*

Hell really isn't something to casually discuss, but I find it sadly interesting how flippant so many people are in the use of the word. I can't tell you how many times I've heard the phrase "Go to hell" thrown at someone who has done or said something rude or offensive on TV. Since it's used in that context, there's an understated comprehension that hell is a bad place for bad people. But the truth is that people honestly don't have a clue what hell is actually like. They really don't.

The popular 90s sitcom *Seinfeld* sums up the general public's vision of hell quite nicely in an episode where Elaine finds out that her boyfriend, David Puddy, is a Christian by finding a Jesus fish on the back of his car. In a subsequent conversation with him, she quickly learns that Puddy not only thinks she is going to hell but that he doesn't seem to care too much about it. This upsets Elaine, even though she doesn't even believe in hell's existence. The conversation goes like this:

Elaine: David! I'm going to hell! The worst place in the world… with devils, and those caves, and the ragged clothing!

Puddy: It's gonna be rough.

Elaine: You should be trying to save me!

Puddy: Don't boss me! This is why you're going to hell.

Elaine: I am not going to hell…and if you think I'm going to hell, you should care that I'm going to hell even though I am not!

Not only does Elaine get upset by the fact that Puddy thinks she is going to a horrible place she doesn't believe in, she's even more irate because Puddy isn't proactive at trying to rescue her from that terrible (albeit fictional to her) place.

The first time that I saw this episode, I knew that it had hit the nail right on the head in a couple of ways. It (a) humorously portrays the indifference of so many Christians accurately, and most importantly, (b) captures the reaction of a nonbeliever to a "believer" when they just don't care enough to act, even though eternity happens to be on the line.

Elaine's major problem with Puddy is that he won't share with her the way to escape from the clutches of hell. If it's something he truly believes in, he should speak up and be intentional about saving her…but he doesn't. Because of Puddy's apathy, Elaine feels neglected and unloved.

I know all of this might seem a bit silly, but do you find yourself in the same unconcerned camp as David Puddy sometimes? I hate to admit it, but I find myself there all too often. Many, many people out there don't believe that hell even exists. But if we aren't doing anything about it, they have every right to be upset with us. Why? Because hell *does* exist. People who don't know Christ will spend eternity there. You and I should care.

The cartoonish misconception of hell - that it is like the edge of a volcano with caves and little devils running around with pitchforks - has tricked a large proportion of society into believing that even if it does exist, it's not all that bad. The bible describes hell as being a place of darkness, weeping, and the complete absence of God. That truth is something that should shatter the caricatured image and grip our hearts to move toward action.

The only hope people have is in Christ alone - and we need to tell them that. Hell is no laughing matter and the Evil One has attempted to defuse the horrific reality of hell through a humorous interpretation of it. Don't fall for it the way so many others have. Sharing your faith is so much more important than you know because the reaction to our message has eternal consequences. Even though it may be awkward to publically talk to others about what we privately believe, the message we have to share is extremely important.

People don't really know what they're saying when they angrily shout, "Go to hell!" to another individual who has wronged them. And the only way they'll find out the truth is if we tell them.

Part of Elaine's view of Christians is correct, and her expression of anger toward Puddy might make you want to respond in a way that would change her perception of us. If so, that's great...because answering the question of whether or not we truly care that people will go to hell if they don't know Christ tells us a lot about what is going on inside of our hearts. If your answer doesn't sit right, ask God to soften your heart toward those that need Him and pray for the kind of compassion that God has for the lost that need to be found. You'll be amazed how He will refine your outlook.

26
JACK, VOLDEMORT, AND VICTORIA (The British Woman Who Lives Inside My GPS)

The fact that I am a miserable sinner reveals itself to me multiple times a day, every day of the week. I am selfish. I am lazy. And like any self-absorbed American, I want instant gratification. If I cannot have something that I want right now, it makes me want it all the more.

Example: the time I have the greatest desire to consume a Chick-Fil-A sandwich is on Sunday, the only day that Chick-Fil-A is closed. Something alerts me on that day like a biological clock and I just gotta get me some nuggets and waffle fries. When I come to the realization that it is closed, I inevitably get super annoyed at the restaurant chain and say something like, "Why are they closed on Sundays? Who are they trying to impress by taking today off? God? We're under the New Covenant and this religious activity in order to gain the Lord's acceptance does nobody any good. Especially me!"

See what I mean? I am a wicked and rotten sinner, completely selfish in my flesh. Time after time when I mess up, I'll come to this awful realization of how horrible I'm behaving and say to myself, "Shelby, what is wrong with you? This is incompatible with who you are at the core of your spiritual center."

It's almost like a battle is taking place inside me. On one side is the noble Jack Bauer from *24*, fighting for what's good and right, while the other side is the sinister Voldemort from *Harry Potter*, trying to destroy any glimpse of goodness and take every bit of control for himself. With a continuous battle of two competent opponents taking place inside of me all the time, there is an ever-flowing tension at the very center of who I really am. This battle unavoidably spawns questions like, "How can I possibly be a great example for Jesus when in my mind, I just cussed out the Christian founder of Chick-Fil-A for honoring the Lord's Day?"[28]

Let me attempt to illustrate this pattern of behavior in my heart by describing the relationship that I used to have with Victoria, the British woman who lives inside the GPS device I once used in my car. After I received a Global Positioning System for Christmas a few years ago, I immediately opened it up and chose the female voice with the UK accent to be my audible guide through the roads and highways of these United States.

I went with the woman's voice because I didn't want a dude telling me where to go when I was lost (reminded me too much of my Middle School PE teacher who yelled at just about everyone). And I selected the British option because any person with an accent from London's West End instantly sounds intelligent.[29] Seriously. You can make scripts from old episodes of *Gossip Girl* sound utterly brilliant when they are read with an British accent. Lastly, I decided to name her Victoria because the last person I met from the UK was a Christian musician named Vicki Beeching, so that seemed to fit.[30]

Anyway, Victoria and I became fast friends as she helped me get places I needed to go and I conversed with her on long car trips to places like Morgantown, West Virginia (I'm pretty sure no British people live there).

"At the end of the road, turn right. Then, take the motorway," she would say to me as I responded with, "Oh, Victoria. It's called a highway, you silly Brit."

She was always aware of the proper way to get me to my destination and all was well with us as long I was obedient to her benevolent directions. That satellite in the sky was her way of knowing whether or not I was being compliant to her bearings, and if I happened to miss a turn or intentionally disobeyed her direct commands, she informed me of the most suitable way to remedy my faults.

"Turn around when possible," she would politely say if I was going the wrong way. So I usually did.

But every now and then, I would feel like I knew a better way to get someplace than she did, so I would intentionally ignore her instructions, usually placing me smack in the middle of nowhere, 26 miles off the beaten path. When I would come to my senses and swallow my pride, I readjusted my course to Victoria's specifications and she would gently instruct me on the correct path to my goal.

When we would arrive, she'd always triumphantly exclaim, "You have reached your destination," and I would either be happy that I had arrived on schedule or embarrassed by my tardiness because of my stubborn self-will.

If I decided to take an alternate route that didn't line up with Victoria's benevolent intentions for my travel, my reaction was always the same. I'd keep glancing at the GPS screen, knowing that I was not going to be following the long red arrow to the next turn or exit. My palms would get a little sweaty, and in a sense, I would feel guilty for not being obedient to this synthesized voice inside an electronic box on my dashboard. Something inside of me wanted to try and get back to the proper path she had instructed me to take, but another part of me thought that I was right in going my own way.

OK, here's what I'm getting at—there is a constant battle inside of my heart on whether to do the right thing or to do the wrong thing. The end of Romans 7 puts it this way:

So I find this law at work: When I want to do good, evil is right there with me. For in my inner being I delight in God's law; but I see another law at work in the members of my body, waging war against the law of my mind and making me a prisoner of the law of sin at work within my members. What a wretched man I am! Who will rescue me from this body of death? Thanks be to God—through Jesus Christ our Lord! So then, I myself in my mind am a slave to God's law, but in the sinful nature a slave to the law of sin.

In a way, it's good to know that the ultimate stud of the faith (the apostle Paul) struggled with the same thing that I do, day in and day out.

The truth is that every believer has a Jack Bauer and Voldemort inside of them, battling it out for control of their actions and thoughts. Sometimes Voldemort draws his wand and casts the killing curse at the chest of Jack Bauer, leaving him lifeless, with evil triumphing in the moment. Yet sometimes, Jack Bauer pulls his sidearm and puts two bullets in the head of He-Must-Not-Be-Named, rendering evil dead and God glorified in that point in time.

In Romans 7:24, Paul rhetorically asks, "Who can rescue me from this body of death?" So in the language we've been using, it's like saying, "How can I make sure that Jack Bauer always wins over Voldemort when it comes to following the good guidance of Victoria inside the GPS?"

Paul answers his own question in verse 25: "Thanks be to God—through Jesus Christ our Lord!" According to Paul, Christ is clearly the answer to the nagging question of "How do I see victory in my life?"

There will be many moments when you as a believer will be tempted to let Voldemort win when the thickness of this world's values swallow you up and cater to the sinful desires inside your heart. The only real way to keep that from happening is by trusting in the message of the gospel to get you through.

It's been said that we need to preach the gospel to ourselves every day, for by the power of the gospel we will have victory over sin. This is true.

Yes, accepting Christ's death and resurrection to pay for your sin is how you entered into an initial relationship with God. But don't be tempted to think that the power of the gospel stops there. You are in desperate need of that power to get you through every year, every month, every day and every moment. Without it, you are powerless to defeat the evil that resides in the world around you and the flesh within you…and tapping into that power comes by faith. You became a Christian by faith; you walk with God every day by faith. Faith is the nucleus of everything that represents Christianity for "without faith, it is impossible to please God." (Hebrews 11:6)

The battle will go on inside of you and me until the day we breathe our last breath. But until then, I'd personally love to see myself characterized by a life of faith, illustrated with the silhouette of Jack Bauer standing over the corpse of Voldemort on a moment-by-moment basis.

27
JASON BOURNE AND JIM HALPERT

I'm a big fan of extremes. When I hear that a circus-style catch happened in a baseball game the day before, I'll immediately go online to see the replay. Additionally, if I ever flip by the TLC network and there's an hour-long show about a dude weighing 1000 lbs., you know that (at the very least) I'll be DVR-ing that sucker to watch again and again.

For some reason, my instinct is to be drawn to extreme action or to extreme lethargy. I couldn't tell you why, though. Swinging the pendulum to either side strikes some bizarre chord in me that satisfies an intrinsic desire to have everything be far-fetched.

I guess that's why I can be enamored with someone like Jason Bourne at the same time I'm captivated by Jim Halpert.

Jason Bourne is a fictional character created by novelist Robert Ludlum and brought to life in *The Bourne* series of novels, which were later turned into three kick-butt movies starring Matt Damon.[31] If you've read the books or seen the movies, you know what kind of person Bourne is—intelligent, fast, competent, trained, intentional, and awesome. Jason Bourne could be the template for the ultimate male: he is goal-driven, constantly moving, proficient in any kind of battle that crosses his path, and, if necessary, he can kill you with a hand towel.

Jim Halpert, on the other hand, is nothing like Jason Bourne, but still very cool. Jim Halpert is the laid-back, slow-moving, lanky, and somewhat passive character from NBC's *The Office*. He takes life as it comes, has a fantastic sense of humor, takes pride in mediocre work, and is an all-around "chill" personality. Much of his disposition is a direct result of his mundane work environment, but nevertheless, I often find myself wanting to be just like Jim.

I probably wouldn't be too far off if I said that many Christian personalities out there are a lot like mine in regard to my silly desires to be like Jason Bourne or Jim Halpert...specifically when it comes to the area of connecting with the culture at large. I hold this opinion mostly because a lot of the Christians I know have a strong urge to swing the pendulum to one side or the other on the issues that rise up when we read pieces of Scripture like 1 Corinthians 9:19-23.

Though I am free and belong to no man, I make myself a slave to everyone, to win as many as possible. To the Jews I became like a Jew, to win the Jews. To those under the law I became like one under the law (though I myself am not under the law), so as to win those under the law. To those not having the law I became like one not having the law (though I am not free from God's law but am under Christ's law), so as to win those not having the law. To the weak I became weak, to win the weak. I have become all things to all men so that by all possible means I might save some. I do all this for the sake of the gospel, that I may share in its blessings.

To be honest, both extremes that bubble up from this piece of Scripture and surface in Christian circles are rather irritating. These extremes are known as *legalism* and *license*. Let me explain what I mean.

Many believers have a tendency to ignore a Bible passage like this because either they don't understand it or it doesn't fit in to their comfortable religious lifestyle.

Martin Luther once said, "Religion is the default of the human heart." True. We tend to find comfort in routine, order, and "doing things right" because it makes us feel better about ourselves and lets us draw comparisons between us and the people that just get it wrong. In short, everybody - in one form or another - is religious. Then, some people take it to the next level and throw God into the mix. Acting religious for religion's sake is really easy to do when you think that God will love you more and people will applaud you more if you behave correctly (i.e. don't do what "the world" does).

Scripture like the above passage simply doesn't fit well into a legalistic, religious lifestyle where piety reigns supreme and failure to fall in line results in shame, judgment, condemnation, and resentment. In case you couldn't tell, I've had a lot of experience with this position of legalism, both from others and that which was self-inflicted.

The other side of the coin, however, is just that: a completely opposite approach to the aforementioned lifestyle. Many Christians will read a passage like this and embrace the idea of being all things to all people as a passport to ungodly living. That's legitimate, right?

Uh, no. The text in 1 Corinthians 9 is in no way a "Step Up to the Sin Plate and Take a Swing" invitation to the follower of Christ. The key here to understanding the significance of verse 23: "I do this all for the sake of the gospel..."

You don't get drunk for the sake of the gospel. You don't lead a sexually promiscuous lifestyle for the sake of the gospel. If you think you're honoring God by doing those kinds of things in the name of "connecting with culture," you might be crazy.

Probably the best way to interpret the apostle Paul's intent in writing this passage is by using (you guessed it) more scripture. Check this out:

Make every effort to live in peace with all men and to be holy; without holiness no one will see the Lord.
HEBREWS 12:14

There are two commands here that I want to highlight.

The first command: "live in peace with all men." Basically, connect with culture. Understand what people love, what makes them happy, sad, frustrated, or joyful. What do non-Christians "pound the table" about? Find out what it is so that you can be educated enough to engage in conversation with them and talk about the things that they want to talk about.

The second command: "be holy." Walk uprightly and dwell in the light. Be set apart from the norm and live your life differently than what the world says it should look like. Be holy.

Now, put those two together and this is what you get—balance your life by being *connected* to the culture but not *immersed* in it. In other words, be *in* the world but not *of* the world. That's what it means to make yourself a slave to everyone in order to win as many as possible for the sake of the gospel. It's not about disconnecting yourself from the culture and it's not about mimicking the ungodly lifestyle of those who don't know Christ. It's about drawing a healthy balance between being at peace with all people and living a holy life.

And don't forget the end of the 1 Corinthians text either: "...that I may share in its blessings." What a privilege it is to be messengers of the gospel and share in its blessings. I can't believe that God chooses to involve awkward-me in what He's doing in the lives of people who don't yet know Him.

Although I may want to model myself after Jason Bourne and Jim Halpert, the truth is that I'm probably better off residing somewhere in the middle of those two personalities. I can't really think of a character who would live up to that perfection of balance, so I'll just go ahead and say that Jesus Christ is the best model.

Not a bad blueprint to imitate, huh?

28
LIFE IN SWEAT PANTS

People can live 100 years and they don't really live a minute. Climb up here with me, and it's one less minute you haven't lived.
LOGAN HUNTZBERGER TO RORY GILMORE, *GILMORE GIRLS: SEASON 5*

Have you ever had one of those days when you just wore sweat pants? It's kind of chilly outside; maybe it's raining. You wake up and go straight for the hot beverage instead of the shower. Minutes in those sweat pants quickly form into hours and all of a sudden, it's 4:30pm and you feel like a complete waste of space.

Sweat pants automatically create an interesting dilemma, in my line of thinking. For one, I love the kind of comfort they provide me in the cold winter months when I choose not to invade society and stay in my home. There's no way that I'll be putting on jeans if I know I won't be exiting my abode any time soon.

It's also true, however, that if my entire day has been spent wearing said sweat pants, I am ultimately struck with an overwhelming sense of self-loathing that can only be cured by a hot shower, a gummy vitamin supplement, and a quick drive around town with denim on my legs...just to feel like I've actually done something with my life in that 24 hour period.

I guess what I'm trying to say is that I appreciate comfort, but when it comes in self-prescribed high doses, it feels wrong and I get antsy. I think the sinful default setting in my heart is to constantly desire a life of ease - and I'm pretty sure that desire is shared by many other "normal" Americans as well. But in my heart of hearts, I know that a life of continual comfort is just a slack-bottom approach to existence altogether (maybe you know this too).

When we are welcomed into God's family, we are given a purpose that is beyond us. This purpose involves us actively communicating about our faith to others around us. Sure, it's scary, risky, and Lord knows awkward. And every time, it involves us killing that default comfort setting that seems to be so prevalent inside of us.

I have never been 100% comfortable when I am flat-out intentionally living in the world and not of the world, but I'll tell you this: I never feel more alive than when I do. I'm excited, scared, happy, nervous, warm, and intimidated all at once. My mouth is usually dry, my palms are usually wet, and my heart beats faster than when I'm on the elliptical for 45 minutes at Level 6. It's never easy to do, but regardless of how any potential conversation turns out, I always seem to walk away with a renewed sense of purpose and energy.

On more than one occasion after I've stood solidly as a living example of my faith, I have said out loud, "I feel so alive right now."

As a follower of Jesus Christ, all of your life is not meant to be lived in the comfort of flying under the radar and remaining silent about your faith, just as all of your life is not meant to be lived only wearing sweat pants. Maybe it's time that you slipped on a pair of jeans and left the sweat pants behind for a while so that you might experience the kind of life Jesus promises here:

...I have come that they may have life, and have it to the full.
JOHN 10:10B

29
THE AMAZING REALLY GOODS

Even though I'm only 5'6" tall and weigh a buck forty soaking wet, I'm a surprisingly good athlete out on the flag football field. Really, I am; don't snicker.

A few years ago, I was part of a flag football team known simply as "The Amazing Really Goods." That's such a great team name, isn't it? Our desire was to have a title that would send a message to all those opponents we would face out there...and that message was: we're amazing and we're really good.

One year, our season of hard work landed us smack dab in the middle of the championship for the coveted title of "Division 2 Intramural Flag Football Champions of the South East Region." This was a title that we did not take lightly.

For our final game, we were playing a team called "Ricky Williams' Secret Stash," which gave me a pretty good understanding of what these dudes did on a typical Saturday night. Rumor had it that they were pretty tough out on the football field though, so I remember being very nervous during pre-game warm-ups. Looking around at my teammates as we stretched, I could see that all of them were feeling exactly the same thing that I was feeling...all of them except for Matt. He looked totally at peace with the world and unnaturally calm, considering the fact that we were about to play in the most important game of the year.

Let me tell you a little bit about Matt. See, he was a senior in the Army ROTC program at school and he had just returned home from a 12-month stint in Iraq, literally fighting for our country.

While overseas, Matt carried a weapon and sometimes he even had to use it. He saw explosions, screaming women and children in pain, tanks, humvees, blood, and sand. Good friends of his got shot and he was even shot at himself on occasion. In everyone's eyes, Matt was a hero who had just come back from war. No one debated that.

And now here we stood—together on a silly intramural flag football field—me feeling nervous and scared while Matt looked as serene as if he were on vacation in the Caribbean.

The game started. We played hard and the outcome was close, but sadly, we ended up losing to the pot-smokers in the end. I remember how frazzled we all were when we were defeated. Some guys left the field without speaking a word and others held their heads low…but again, not Matt.

Matt was lighthearted afterward. He skipped across the field and picked up his bag while throwing an arm around a friend and playfully punching him. He tossed the football back and forth with a few other friends, and joyfully made his way back to his car in the parking lot.

I was completely puzzled at the time and I asked myself the question, "How can he be so cavalier about the fact that we just lost the biggest game of the season?" I didn't get it.

Well, it only took me a few days to figure out what was going on in Matt's mind the night we lost. The answer was simple: to him, it truly was only a game. The Intramural Flag Football Championship was so small in comparison to the things he experienced in the thick of battle only a few months previous. Matt had gone through war, so why get so upset about something that was supposed to be just fun competition?

You know, I think a lot about Matt and his experiences when I think about a Christian who is characterized by being in the world but not of the world. In many ways, when we are out there on the front lines of battle for God's Kingdom sharing our faith and living authentic Christianity, the other annoying little details of life begin to slip into their rightful place behind what's really important.

When I'm active in putting others first for the sake of the gospel and standing up for the integrity of what it means to be a follower of Jesus, suddenly (for example) traffic doesn't bother me as much as it used to. The small things in life truly become smaller in light of the fact that people die every day without knowing Jesus.

I now understand why Matt was the way he was at the game that night. I only wish that I could continue to have that kind of proper perspective on life when it comes to majoring in the majors and letting the minors be the minors during my years on this planet. Our time here is short and God calls us to live in light of eternity.

Someone very wise once told me that all of life is about perspective. And when I'm living the authentic Christian life or sharing my faith on a regular basis, my perspective is vividly accurate. Why? Because I'm focused on the things that are most important in light of all eternity. I don't sweat the details and I don't lose my cool over stuff that, in the grand scheme of things, just doesn't matter as much. Matt was a good guy who held a great perspective that I can continue to learn from.

Now if I could only go back and change the outcome of that flag football game.

I'm kidding…no I'm not.

30
EFFECTS OF A TYPHOON

When a boy reaches a certain age in life, the world (as it's been said) is his oyster. Now, I don't really care for seafood, so I'm not quite sure what that means. I do know, however, that I loved life when I was ten years old.

At that particular age, my boyhood was defined by everything that was adventurous and muddy. I climbed trees, fell off my bike and skinned my knees, threw rocks at bees' nests, dug for treasure in the backyard, and even buried my own head in the sand once (true story). And in the middle of my pre-adolescent years, I was blessed enough to have the adventure quotient ratcheted up to the next level by my dad receiving a military stationing assignment on the tropical island of Guam.

In case you're unaware, Guam is a little island way out in the Pacific Ocean, just above the equator, that is an American territory. We lived there for two years and I have nothing but fond memories for the tiny little paradise that could probably be completely carpeted by the Home Depot for $135.

As a child, I did know that Guam was a place of exotic excitement and exhilarating adventure, but what I didn't know was that the island was no stranger to these crazy storms called typhoons. A typhoon, for you land-locked Americans, is essentially a hurricane on crack.

Well, you probably guessed it already, but in the winter of our first year there, Typhoon Roy hit the island of Guam...and he hit it hard. All of our house windows were boarded up, trees were blown over and uprooted, coconuts flew through the air and smashed into car windshields, rain fell at monsoon levels, and the power was inevitably lost from the island for days.

I'll never forget that first night in the house together as a family after Roy paid us a visit. I found myself standing at the dining room table with my mom and sister, putting together a 1000 piece jigsaw puzzle by candlelight and listening to the nasty destruction-producing storm raging outside. Now, the average 10 year old boy is brave when it comes to garden variety adventure around the house, but I've got to admit that Typhoon Roy scared me half to death. Every creak, bump, and bang I heard outside made me jump with fright and fear for what might happen if our window shutters didn't hold up against the wind. Needless to say, I was terrified.

Well, after about 50 pieces into the puzzle, my bladder got the best of me. I needed to go, which meant one more frightening thing—walking to the bathroom at the back of the house by myself in the darkness. In that moment, I thought about just peeing my pants so that I didn't have to leave the safety of the candlelight, but I knew that kids my age didn't voluntarily do that anymore. So I manned up, grabbed the flashlight on the kitchen counter, and made my way to the back of the house, one shaky footstep at a time.

When I reached the entrance to the hallway that led to the bathroom, I stopped and noticed how very dark the hallway appeared and that, in the dim flashlight illumination, our clothes hamper at the end of the hallway looked remarkably like one of those tree goblins from the movie *Troll 2*. That, I knew, was just my imagination. But what I heard next was not a creation of my mind: it was something very real.

A strange noise came from around my feet and startled me to the point of jumping backwards, away from the hallway's entrance. Was it our lazy house cat, Muffin, looking for a back scratch or Tender Vittles packet? I couldn't be sure, so I reluctantly let my flashlight fall to the ground near my feet toward where the sound was coming from.

What I saw next changed my perspective on everything that was running through my mind that night and probably gave me the ability to recall this story with as much vivid detail as I can now. The narrow beam of light quickly revealed my dad in full workout gear, covered in sweat and doing pushups on the carpeted floor.

See, at that time in his life, my dad was a marathon runner and if he wasn't able to get outside to run (like, if there was a typhoon, for example), he would workout at home by doing sit-ups, pushups, and stretching exercises. I came across him, smack in the middle of his in-home workout. When my flashlight lit up my dad in that moment, I remember this immediate wave of comfort that swept over my mind and body. I wasn't afraid of the dark hallway anymore. The sounds of the storm outside didn't scare me as much as they did a few minutes ago. The clothes hamper at the end of the hall was just a piece of wicker furniture.

As I saw my dad doing pushups on the floor that night, looking all manly and tough, I took solace in the fact that he would protect me from the dangers going on outside. He wouldn't let any monster that lurked in the darkness grab my legs and gobble me up. He would care for me if any harm would befall me. My fears recoiled in the light of his protection and strength because I knew one thing: my dad loved me.

As an adult now, I look back on this story as a wonderful example of how much God loves and cares for me. When I was a kid, I knew that my dad would protect me from anything that tried to harm me, and my anxiety that night was vanquished the second I saw him exercising on the floor. My dad is a great example of earthly love and protection, but God is infinitely more loving and caring than any earthly father could be. The evidence is here:

So if you sinful people know how to give good gifts to your children, how much more will your heavenly father give good gifts to those that ask him?
MATTHEW 7:11

Many of us constantly struggle with worry, anxiety, and paralyzing fear. Those emotions can color our lives if we let them, but God calls us as His children to something much better than time-wasting worry. If we look to our Heavenly Father in all of His strength and love, our anxiety will melt like a crayon in the sun because we *know* that He loves us and wants what is best for us. It may not be immediately apparent, but we can always look to our Father as a way to alleviate the anxiety that has a nasty habit of sitting in the driver's seat of our lives.

Typhoon Roy brought not only destruction to Guam that year, but it also brought fear to the heart of a little boy who then quickly recognized his dad was a safeguard in the midst of the chaos. If we recognize that God is, in fact, God and that He is *for* us, not *against* us, worry will diminish in our lives and leave room for growth, faith, and intimacy with our Father. That can only lead to good things, as we become a visible example to anyone wondering what it really means to be a Christian with authentic faith in a world that constantly exalts the shallow and honors the trite.

We may always feel somewhat awkward living in the world, but when others see how much we trust our heavenly Father, they will naturally be drawn to something that is much deeper than what they experience in their lives.

31
GIRL MEETS RHINO

Let me tell you about my all-time favorite TV commercial. It was for the St. Paul Insurance Company and the images in it were powerful enough to burn the message it was communicating into my brain before the company logo was even displayed.

It opens with a shot of a little white girl with curly blond hair, wearing a blue dress and standing in the middle of the African savannah. She's all by herself, holding a long blade of grass and looking completely out of place because she seems to be dressed for Sunday School as opposed to a safari.

Next the camera flashes to something else in that same field, a distance away. It's not a little girl this time, but a full-grown rhinoceros.

The camera focuses again on the little girl, who turns and looks at the rhino in the distance... and seems completely unimpressed by its presence. The rhino, on the other hand, catches sight of the girl, snorts with anger, and begins to charge in her direction.

The girl sees this and does nothing. She remains completely motionless as the rhino runs right at her, moving faster and faster.

The huge creature continues to gain speed and soon the camera meets in the middle as the charging beast quickly closes in on her. As it does, a large cloud of dust completely fills the screen, preventing you from seeing the anticipated carnage.

However, the dust quickly clears and the rhino is standing there, motionless, right next to the little girl, who is totally unharmed. She looks right at the camera, smiles, and giggles a little...then she reaches out and rubs the rhino's horn like it's the family puppy. No big deal.

The screen then fades to black and the tagline for the commercial appears:

Trust is not being afraid, even if you are vulnerable.

After I first saw this commercial, I remember thinking, *Wow, that is so accurate!* Not that a rhino and a little girl would ever be together in a situation like that, of course, but the tagline. "Trust is not being afraid, even if you are vulnerable." That sentence has been indelibly written on my heart and mind ever since.

When I choose to live my life as an unashamed and awkward Christian on display for others to see, I am vulnerable. I open myself up for ridicule, and being labeled a religious zealot or creator of all things awkward in conversation. I run that risk every time I choose to speak up about the name of Jesus Christ.

But if I believe in the One who calls me to reach out to others with the message and love of the gospel as an example for all to see, I don't need to be afraid. Why? Because I trust in His goodness. I trust in His power. I trust in His ability to do amazing and eternal things in other people's lives through someone that is as thoroughly awkward as I am. And that gives me the confidence to know that it really isn't about my eloquence or brilliant responses to profound questions. It isn't necessarily about how great I am at saying the right thing at the right time and making sure I live my life perfectly so that I can be the ultimate example of a follower of Christ.

It's about trusting that God can bring people to Himself if I step out in faith and make myself vulnerable. 1 Corinthians 2:3-5 says this about what God can do in spite of who we are:

I came to you in weakness and fear, and with much trembling. My message and my preaching were not with wise and persuasive words, but with a demonstration of the Spirit's power, so that your faith might not rest on men's wisdom, but on God's power.

Beautiful, isn't it? God chooses to use us in our weakness to prove how strong He is. Why? So the recognition and glory can go to God and never be mistaken as something achieved by the feeble power of my humanity.

In the Old Testament, we are given another example of this via Psalm 8:2:

> *Out of the mouth of babies and infants, you have established strength because of your foes, to still the enemy and the avenger.*
> ESV

Isn't that cool? God can use the babbling words of infants and babies to demonstrate the kind of power He has over everything. What is more lightweight than the nonsensical ramblings of infant children? I have a baby, so trust me; the answer is "nothing." And God says here that He is capable of manifesting His strength to still His enemies through that kind of medium. More proof that God uses the weak to communicate how strong He is.

A friend of mine once told me that God uses crooked sticks to draw straight lines. It really is quite incredible that the Creator of the universe chooses to involve us in what He is doing to show Himself off and reconcile people to Himself. Miserable, messed up, selfish people like us are the tools (crooked sticks) that God chooses to use in His divine plan to redeem mankind (straight lines)…all we have to do is make ourselves available.

Trust is not being afraid, even if you're vulnerable.

PART FOUR

THINGS THAT HELP YOU GET THINGS DONE

INTRODUCTION: THE METHODS (Some Specific How-To's)

Methods are many, principles are few.
Methods can change, but principles never do.
WARREN WIERSBE

Honestly, some people make Christianity and the message of the gospel look about as attractive as an airport smoking lounge. Wait, do those things still exist?

Anyway, the methods by which we communicate the greatest message ever known to humankind are extremely important because those methods are capable of breaking down pre-existing walls that might prevent others from understanding the purity of the gospel. However, those methods are also capable of *creating* additional barriers that obstruct a clear pathway to comprehending the truth. So the "how" is an incredibly significant variable when we choose to proactively be in the world but not of it.

It's essentially Communication 101: walk the walk and present the message with clarity, so it will be received in the way that was intended by the original source. In short, live the Christian life with integrity and communicate the gospel truth with relevance, using whatever approach helps people best understand it. In order to make this happen, we must be "others-centered."

Of course, not all people absorb information in the same way, so it's vital that we learn how to communicate the same message in a variety of ways in order to reach as many as possible for the glory of God. The methods may change on how to communicate the message, but always remember that the gospel is an everlasting constant. It must always be the horizon line we keep our eye on when the conditions are constantly changing around us.

Think of this section as a kind of tool belt: some specifics on how to be in the world but not of it, as a speaker *for* and representative *of* Jesus Christ.

32
DEATH OF A PRAIRIE DOG

Every now and then I'll see, hear, or smell something that will remind me of a specific moment from my past. Depending on whether the history is good or bad can alter my current mood in a very significant way. Isn't it weird how memories are capable of doing that?

I'm a person who often reflects on childhood remembrances and stories of good times with friends and family, but I'm not going to lie and tell you that all of those recollections are clearly vivid. I have been known to screw up a few of the details every now and then, which can make some stories sound funnier or more dramatic than they really were. As true as that may be for many of my tales from the past, it is simply not the case for this one. Everything that I'm about to tell you is absolutely true and the details have not been exaggerated or skewed to make for a more interesting story. Get ready, because this is my account of the death of a prairie dog.

When I was about 15 years old, I went on a camping trip with my sister, my ex-Step Mom, and her current boyfriend, who later became her husband. (This is a story in and of itself, but I'm not going to go there right now.) It was approaching the end of a summertime trip of seeing most of my extended family in California and I decided to take this camping trip with the aforementioned group of people to a lake in Oregon before the vacation was over.

Now, once we got there, we weren't really going to rough it in tents or anything like that, because we had a huge pop-up fifth wheel camper in tow, complete with kitchen, shower, and one of those toilets you have to hook up to a giant hose to empty when you exit the campsite (think cousin Eddie from *National Lampoon's*

Christmas Vacation). So this was a "camping" trip in the loosest of terms (but I have no regrets about sleeping on a bed away from blood-sucking insects when I get the chance).

When we completed the drive up north and pulled into the campground, the beauty of the area literally took my breath away. There were cedar trees that seemed taller than skyscrapers and the lake was the clearest I had ever seen in my life. There were small fields of clover and wildflowers, populated by deer and birds that literally came up to humans and ate tiny scraps of bread from the hands of children. And the coolest thing of all to me were the hundreds of prairie dogs that skittered through the patches of flowers, dodging tree roots and diving into their subterranean homes.

Before I go on, let me tell you a little something about 15 year-old boys: they're idiots. Truly, they are. When we stopped the truck and hopped out to take in the view of the land, the first thing that went through my 15 year-old mind was not, "Wow, this place is gorgeous!" Instead, it was, "Hmm, I wonder how many times I could throw a rock at a prairie dog before I could hit it?"

I'll say it again—15 year-old boys are idiots.

We quickly settled in to our campsite and got situated enough to feel like home for a few days before each of us decided to go exploring on our own for a few minutes. I took this time to immediately make a B-line for the nearest patch of clover, in hot pursuit of my prairie dog prey.

On my way, I bent down and randomly picked up four or five medium-sized rocks that I thought were just the right shape and weight to hurl at a speeding animal the size of a large rat. When I got to the first mini-field of clover and flowers, I widened my stance a bit and stood silently like a sumo wrestler on the edge of a ring, ready to pounce as soon as the situation called for it. Only a couple of minutes went by before I saw a prairie dog pop up out of a hole in the ground and start darting across the field, away from where I was standing.

A starting gun went off in my mind and I sprang forward toward the little thing like a teenage girl chasing down Robert Pattinson in a parking lot. When the prairie dog spotted me running after it, he kicked it into high gear and darted away from me with the kind of haste that can only be described as "awe-inspiring." It was now or never for me, so as I was in mid-stride, I plucked a single rock from the cluster of them in my left hand, cocked back my entire right arm, and chucked the stone toward the prairie dog like a Major League Baseball pitcher.

What happened next seemed like it occurred in slow motion. The rock flew through the air, top over bottom toward the little guy on a frozen rope of pinpoint accuracy. Inch by inch, it sailed toward him, finally making stunningly perfect contact at the back of his head, then ricocheting off at a 90 degree angle toward the woods. I think I heard a small "thump" sound in that moment followed by a tiny little, "Nooooo!," but it's possible that I just imagined that part.

The prairie dog instantly flipped over onto his back, put both of his front paws together, and made like he was digging a hole in the air for a few seconds. Then he stopped sharply, froze his paws in mid-air and collapsed onto his left side. When I processed the fact that I had hit the prairie dog on my first throw, I stopped running, dropped the remaining rocks in my hand, lifted both of my fists to the sky and shouted, "I hit him on the first try! All of you woodland creatures bow before me, for I am your KING!"

A couple of mental high-fives and booty shakes later, I walked over to the little guy to gently nudge him from his stunned state, in hopes that he would just shake it off and run back into the closest hole. But what I discovered next would quickly change my prideful attitude and burn this whole experience into my mind for the rest of my life.

Gently tapping him with my shoe didn't wake him. Clapping my hands loudly next to his head didn't make him move. And lightly poking him with a nearby stick didn't make him hop to his feet and scurry away. In that moment, I came to the realization that I had, in fact, killed that precious little prairie dog with a crude rock that I found on nature's floor.

A wave of remorse promptly swept over me. All of the pride and jubilation I felt from my rock-throwing accuracy drained from my body, leaving nothing but guilt and sadness. I couldn't believe that I had actually killed that innocent creature because of an idiotic desire to turn rock-throwing into a game. What had I done? What had I done?

After about ten minutes of self-condemnation, I came up with a plan to make things right. I took the stick I had been holding and dug a hole in the ground, roughly the size of a shoebox. I then stepped over in front of the dead prairie dog and picked him up with my bare hands (I do not recommend this, by the way) and gently laid him inside his final resting place. After covering him with the loose soil I had dug up, I walked over to the nearest patch of wildflowers, picked four or five (ironically the same number of rocks I had initially picked up), and placed them on top of the grave. I then performed a small funeral service that included two full minutes of silence and a genuine heartfelt prayer that went something like this:

Lord, I'm so sorry for murdering one of the creatures you created. Please forgive me. I pray that you would accept this prairie dog into your presence and may he always run freely in the clover fields of glory. Amen.

After the service was over, I felt so much better about myself for handling my mistake in a way that was honorable and good. I was able to enjoy the rest of the camping trip we had in the beautiful state of Oregon, and I vowed never again to throw rocks of any kind at any of God's creatures.

I know this may sound funny to you after a story like this, but we as human beings do this kind of stuff all the time with God. No, I don't mean the whole funeral for a prairie dog thing…I'm talking about the heart attitude of checks and balances. Whenever we foul up and make a mistake that overwhelms us with guilt, we think that our bad thing can be covered up in God's eyes if we do something good. When I was an idiotic fifteen year-old, I quite literally thought that I could cover up my misdeed with a good act of an appropriate burial service. But even today I'm extremely guilty of the "good stuff cancels out bad stuff" belief system in my everyday life. I always think, "If I just feel guilty long enough" or "If I'm nicer to more people today than yesterday" or "If I give more than I gave last time" or "If I read my bible for a little longer today," etc. It may sound ridiculous, but my heart really thinks that these kinds of actions and attitudes can save me from condemnation. How incredibly foolish!

I have yet to find the verse or verses in the bible that say something to the effect of, "Doing one good thing cancels out doing one bad thing, so make sure that you do more good things than bad things or God isn't going to love you and He'll probably send you to hell." Why do we diminish the grace of God to checks and balances? Why do we believe that we can save ourselves from condemnation with a good thought or a good action? Being right with God has nothing to do with our actions and everything to do with the love of God through His Son, Jesus Christ.

If you believe that it's about Jesus and His love, you will live that way, and if you live that way, your life will shine in stark contrast to the kind of life that is enslaved to performance. The world around you will see the difference and be irresistibly drawn to the relationship you have with God.

Connection with Him is about grace through faith, not good action to appease wrath and guilt. We have to stop performing prairie dog funeral services to make ourselves feel better and start living in the truth that a relationship with God cannot be purchased with good works.

33
GAME ON, SUCKA

If I'm in the right mood, I can be easily convinced to join a group of people and play a game. My in-laws are really big game people, and that always makes for a lot of laughs at family gatherings. Most of the time, the humor comes from someone making a Freudian slip and saying something completely inappropriate, causing the entire room to erupt in deep belly laughter.

A few years ago at Christmas, my wife and I gave my brother-in-law a new board game. Not too long after the presents were opened, we gathered together as a group near the still-twinkling Christmas tree and decided to take a crack at some new and healthy competition amongst family. It was a game that none of us had ever played before, so the routine course of action took place before we could all get started and play: we read the rules. Ugh.

Honestly, I absolutely can't stand reading the rules before playing a game. I'm ready to talk smack to my opponents and just get into it, sucka! There is fun to be had and pausing to make sure I engage in the fun correctly kind of saps away most of the excitement for me. The truth is, however, that if someone didn't read the rules first, we would end up playing the game wrong, the scoring wouldn't make any sense, and the actual fun would get derailed by arguments, frustration and someone inadvertently kicking the glass coffee table. I'm quite sure the game would then be off, sucka.

For many areas of life (not just playing board games) the key to fruitfulness is appropriate preparation. And the intentionality of being in the world but not of the world is no exception. Yes, it is important to be ready to answer any specific questions that might come up when you're in a spiritual conversation with someone, but the preparation I'm talking about here has to do with prayer.

If you closely examine the ministry of Jesus, you will easily discover that He was a man who took prayer very seriously. The bible says that Jesus often withdrew to lonely places to pray (Luke 5:16). This is significant; given the fact that He knew His ministry would be relatively short (three years) and packed with activity (teaching, miracles, travel, etc.) A running motto for every Christian should be, "If it's good enough for Jesus, it's good enough for me" (although this doesn't fit on a bracelet quite as well as **WWJD**). Jesus' busy life didn't lack prayer and neither should ours.

Frankly, if we're not praying throughout the entire process of living out our faith in the world, we're trying to accomplish the work of God through our own efforts. Although we might try to make it work in our own power, we simply don't have the capacity to handle the rigors of living a spiritually fruitful life while remaining unaffected by the constant pressures of the world.

Prayer is where our strength comes from, it's where our hearts become aligned with God's, it's where our motivations are focused on the appropriate things and it's where we recognize who is really behind all of this anyway. We need to ask God to open people's hearts to the gospel before we open our mouths. We must be talking to Him about our fears and apprehension in a way that honestly recognizes that He must work in order to bring genuine life change.

Prayer really is the best way to prepare in order to see good things happen. And if your schedule doesn't reveal prayer as the foundation for effective ministry and life change, you need to ask yourself what might be pushing you to skip it and move on to the "action."

In John 17, Jesus sets the precedent of how we are to approach a life lived in the world but not of it – a lot of specific prayer. He prays for Himself, he prays for His disciples, and He prays for other believers. Isn't He the best? You know, it may sound cheesy, but Jesus has inspired me to tattoo this mantra on my mind: before you talk to people about God, talk to God about people. It's a great way to live and be prepared for whatever may cross my path.

Game on, sucka.

34
GOOD NEWS/GOOD DEEDS

Lately, several tragedies that have touched the hearts of our nation, from both far away and close to home. The one that personally impacted me the most was the Virginia Tech shootings in April of 2007. (In case you forgot, I'm a Hokie.)

In recent years, I've been amazed by the outpouring of self-sacrificial response to human suffering (particularly from college students) through people's desire to help, give, serve, work, and go. I remember when thousands of college students gave up their spring breaks to travel down to New Orleans and help clean up the cataclysmic disaster left behind by Hurricane Katrina. It's astounding to me that so many Christians genuinely wanted to help by serving those who had been affected by such a horrible catastrophe. In times like these, it is so important to model Christ's love by physically helping people in the midst of their pain.

Issues like this do create a bit of rub, though. Now, hear me out on this before you close this book and chuck it through the closest window. As disciples of Jesus Christ, God calls us to care for the poor, help widows and orphans, provide aid for the physically afflicted, and love others by serving them in their time of need... as far as I know, not many in God's Kingdom would question or debate that. However, if *all* Christians do is help people with their physical needs and don't address their spiritual ones, we are making a huge mistake.

Yes, good deeds are important. But stopping at good deeds and neglecting to communicate the Good News is a tragedy in and of itself.

Darryl Smith, the National Director of Cru High School once said:

God calls us to love people by helping them out, but listen to me—the Devil doesn't care if people come to hell full or hungry, fat or skinny, naked or clothed. If all we do is help people with their problems, we have missed the mark entirely. I'm not saying we shouldn't be helping to meet people's tangible needs. Christians should be leading the way in that. But if you're not careful, your ministry will become just another agency that helps people for the next 10 or 15 years as God is calling us to help people for all of eternity.

I agree with Darryl Smith wholeheartedly. God has called us as His church to feed, clothe, and care for those in need, but that is not His primary purpose for us. The primary purpose of the church is to share with people the unfathomable riches of Jesus Christ. This is what Scripture says:

Although I am less than the least of all God's people, this grace was given me: to preach to the Gentiles the unsearchable riches of Christ, and to make plain to everyone the administration of this mystery, which for ages past was kept hidden in God, who created all things.
EPHESIANS 3:8-9

And here is the beauty of it all: sharing the glorious riches of Jesus Christ with people is so much easier to do when doorways are opened by the generous giving of our time, money, service, and care. It's doesn't have to be an "either/or" because it's a "both/and." We must never stop at just caring for people and neglect sharing our faith...and we can easily share our faith by caring for people.

So why draw a line in the sand and pick a side? Remember God's will for you and share your faith like crazy, but don't swing the pendulum too far to that side and never care for people in the process. Additionally, you should love and care for people in need, but if all you do is pick up a broom or paint a building and never share with someone how they can spend eternity with God, you've missed the mark.

Proactively think about some ways that you can inject the principle of Good News *and* Good Deeds into your daily life and take the time to balance the two in ways that inherently draw people to the face of God. This is the epitome of being in the world but not of the world. When we balance Good News and Good Deeds appropriately, we are neck-deep in helping the world, telling them how to connect with the Living God, and unashamedly pointing to the reason behind why we do what we do.

35
WON'T YOU BE MY NEIGHBOR?

And pray for us, too, that God may open a door for our message, so that we may proclaim the mystery of Christ, for which I am in chains. Pray that I may proclaim it clearly, as I should. Be wise in the way you act toward outsiders; make the most of every opportunity. Let your conversation be always full of grace, seasoned with salt, so that you may know how to answer everyone.
COLOSSIANS 4:3-6

What exactly does it mean to "be wise in the way you act toward outsiders?" I suspect that there are several answers that any pastor, theologian, or spiritual leader could come up with. Fortunately, like most occasions when Scripture causes us to ask "how" or "why" questions, the answer can be found this way: just keep reading.

"Being wise toward outsiders" and "making the most of every opportunity" are further clarified in verse 6, addressing specifically the kind of words you use when conversing with people that do not know Christ. So we can essentially conclude that the kind of language we use is extremely important when we are talking about our faith...or just talking in general.

This seems to be an obvious principle that a lot of overzealous Christians adopt in their methods of "converting the masses to Christ"—talking. The problem arises, of course, when all Christians do is talk.

In my early years as a young follower of Jesus Christ, talking seemed to be the only thing I knew how to do when it came to trying to persuade others to believe. I did it a lot and I truly think that my heart was in the proper place at the time. However, when all I did was talk, no room was left in my agenda for listening or loving/godly action.

Unfortunately, I made the common mistake that a lot of

Christians make when I read the words "make the most of every opportunity." To me, this meant talking *at* people instead of talking *with* them. Talking *with* them involves listening well and asking good questions. In my attempts to make the most of every opportunity, I neglected to remember the fact that people are not tasks to be accomplished and checked off of a "To-Convert List," but people are people and they deserve to be treated as such in a respectful manner. You would think that I would've understood this basic human principle, but it nevertheless slipped past me.[32]

Treating others with respect is paramount, and this is where the "act" part of "be wise in the way you act" comes in. My thoughts here come to a point of clarity with the simple phrase uttered by the beloved children's show icon, Mr. Rogers, when he said, "Be a good neighbor."

Being a good neighbor means loving people with your actions… being kind to people, listening to people, loving people, caring about people. When something bad happens in their life and tragedy strikes, your name should be one of the first names that pops into their minds when they want to seek counsel or comfort. Why? Because they know that you love them. And you love them because Jesus loves them.

Far too often, followers of Jesus Christ open their mouths and not their homes, wallets, arms, or calendars. We need to love people with not only our words, but also our actions. And when we do that, we pave roads that clear the way for the gospel to come bursting into people's lives with an overwhelming sense of awe that God's hand is in the whole process.

John Piper put it this way:

> *The fact that God is the ultimate and decisive cause in conversion does not mean we are not causal agents in conversion. We are. And as God's*

agents in conversion we aim at it—we choose what we do an
hope that it will be used by God to bring about convers

Did you catch that? What we *do* and *say* are of equal i here. God is the Author of salvation, but we are key characters in the story. We get to be intimately involved agents of God's love for the lost. That is why it is of vital importance that we love others with our actions and our words by sharing the gospel with them.

Take a minute to stop and think about any possible agendas you might have when you think about the non-believers in your life. Of course, you want them to come to know Christ. But do they perceive that you are constantly treating them as a project and not a person? Would they say that you're a good neighbor? If not, there are some specific steps you can take to change their perspective in order to accurately reflect Jesus Christ.

I know of a few churches and ministries that have adopted this verse as their mantra:

We loved you so much that we were delighted to share with you not only the gospel of God but our lives as well, because you had become so dear to us.
I THESSALONIANS 2:8

This is such a great encapsulation of what I'm talking about here. Of course we need to talk with people about our faith, but we need to share our lives with them as well—with delight. That's what it means to genuinely share the love of Christ with people, because that's exactly what Jesus did when he walked the planet.

When you talk with someone *and* share your life with them, your actions follow up your words in a very tangible way, helping people to see that you're not all talk and no action. They will understand that you sincerely, tangibly care about them.

Talking like a good neighbor and behaving like a good neighbor goes a long, long way in the world today. An unselfish life is a life lived in contrast to the standard American way, and speaks volumes to anyone keeping a close eye on the Christian who talks a big game.

36
STORIES

My high school experience wasn't what you would call average. Because my dad was in the Air Force, I moved all the time. On average, we moved every two years and by the time I was preparing for my fourth high school in four years, I couldn't take it anymore. So I made the very tough decision to stay behind and live with a different family my senior year while the nearest and dearest to me moved to Panama, Central America.

Now that year was over. I had graduated from high school and was preparing to spend the summer with my folks in Panama before venturing off to the new world of college life at Virginia Tech.

That summer before college was so great. I spent my days working part time at the airbase post office, stuffing P.O. boxes for below minimum wage. I played basketball with the other kids in the neighborhood, went body surfing at the only black sand beach in the area, and even fell in love with Maria, the Mormon girl who lived next door to my parents. Alas, it never would have worked for Maria and me, as she was preparing to start her freshman year at Brigham Young University in the fall and I was too short for her to take me seriously as a potential "heathen" boyfriend. I am still, to this day, only 5'6" and not Mormon.

The summer ended and I showed up on campus, bronzed by the Panamanian sun, two short days before classes began. I was unable to attend the "essential orientation time" like everyone else because I wasn't in the country. So when I arrived on campus, I was fascinated, overwhelmed, awed, and frightened all at the same time. Fortunately for me, my assigned roommate was a sophomore who showed me where my classes would be once Monday morning came, which I consider the day I began life as an adult.

One of the most incredible times in a person's life, should they be blessed to experience it, is college. When I was there, I loved college so much that I came up with this little phrase for my e-mail signature —"College: The best 4 to 7 years of your life." Okay, I know that's stupid and overused, but I thought it was funny. Plus it communicated how much I wanted my experience to last longer than it actually would.

Life at an institution of higher learning is truly amazing in so many ways, though. At no other point and time of your life are you able to sleep until 11:30 am, get up, put on sweat pants, walk out into public to go get food, bring it back to your room, eat it while you watch TV, and still be considered a normal, hard-working contributor to society.

You can be anyone you want, say anything you want, and do anything you want (within reason, that is). You can reshape everything about yourself and become someone totally different from the person you were in high school. When I arrived on campus for the first time, I remember thinking, *Hey, none of these people know who I am and none of them care that I lettered in cross-country last year but threw up at the end of every race I ran…it's a fresh start for me!*

And it really was.

I never felt any pressure to be someone that I wasn't or compromise my beliefs just because the popular kids said I should. There were so many different subsets of people at my university and I could have chosen to be a part of any one of them. So I did. And it was my choice, no one else's.

This freedom of choice became very clear to me the first time I ventured out to the dining hall to eat my first meal as a college student. As I approached the building, I remember seeing a small group of people out in front of the cafeteria, walking in a circle with soda cans tied by long strings to their legs while chanting, "IT'S NOT FAIR! IT'S NOT FAIR!"

Of course, I had no clue why they were protesting and it was one of the most bizarre things I had ever seen a group of people do, but everybody walking into and out of the dining hall that evening never even gave them a second look. Nobody seemed to think that this was outside the realm of the ordinary behavior…except for me.

I quickly learned that college was a place for self-expression and weird public displays of opinion. Sure, people ruffled feathers and had heated debates about politics and human rights. Students wrote articles in the school newspaper about global warming that sparked fiery debates in classrooms and study groups. But, honestly, everyone seemed pretty content in just "being who they were."

Now, I'm not naïve enough to think that everyone's college experience is like this. I've heard plenty of stories about the continued pressures of fitting in, bad influences, manipulation, and conditional acceptance. And I'm sure that stuff carries itself into all the remaining time periods of a person's life, regardless of your environment. But for me, my liberties as an 18 to 22 year-old were clear. I could be who I wanted to be.

I ate the food I wanted to eat. I spent my time with the people I enjoyed spending time with. I dated the girls I wanted to date (well, sometimes), and studied the things I wanted to learn more about. In short, I did what I wanted to do.

Little did I know that in January of that first year, I would meet the person who would change my life forever. No, I'm not talking about some sappy, romantic thing with a girl. That was later on in my life. In January, I met a man who claimed he would take the punishment that I deserved for every wrong thing I had ever done. I met a man who promised to accept me and be my friend, regardless of how I acted in the future. I met a man who said he would never turn his back on me or reject me. I met a man who challenged me and gave me a mission and a purpose greater than myself. I met a man who ushered me into a communal Kingdom, full of love and restoration.

In the pages of the Bible, this guy called himself the "Son of Man." We know him better today as Jesus Christ, the Son of God, and He was the One who turned my whole perspective about life upside down.

All of a sudden, my existence wasn't just about me and what I wanted to do, think, study, or talk about. Life was about a greater purpose; a purpose that plugged me into what the Creator of the universe was already doing and had been doing since the beginning of humanity—reconciling people to Himself.

He wanted to involve me in this plan in a very specific way and that mantle of responsibility has changed everything about how I live...and changed it for the better.

I love telling people about my personal story. The story of how Christ came into my life and made me a different person who is now in a restored relationship with God—not because of anything I have done, but because of what God has done for me through Jesus.

I've found that my story (or "testimony") is probably the best way to share the gospel with someone. These days, for some reason, everyone loves to hear a story. Stories capture our hearts and imaginations and sometimes even inject a message that rallies us into action. People love to listen to stories about the trials we have gone through, the spiritual mountaintops we've been on and the lessons life has taught us. I've learned that there is no more personal way to communicate the gospel with someone than by sharing your story with them.

Your story is authentically and uniquely "you." It's not a debate, it's not pushy, it's not fake, and it doesn't feel like religious propaganda because it's coming from your heart. Very rarely will someone argue with you about your own story. In fact, they are more likely to engage you and ask clarifying questions, which in turn pushes the dialogue about Jesus to another more personal level.

If you've never thought about preparing and communicating your story with anyone, that's fine; most Christians haven't. To help you get started, let me give you a few quick and simple guidelines to point you in the right direction.

Guidelines For Sharing Your Story

1. **Keep it short.** Anything longer than 3-5 minutes begins to lose short attention spans. You shouldn't go into the finer points of what you learned as a child in church before summarizing your trials as a middle-schooler before talking about the mistakes you made as a teenager before BLAH, BLAH, BLAH. We all love talking about ourselves, but remember that the purpose of telling your story is not about you, it's about the listener. And, unfortunately, listeners today have a very low tolerance for long-windedness. Remember the 5 B's of public speaking: Be Brief, Baby, Be Brief.

2. **Have a theme.** The theme in my testimony is "freedom/ performance" and I keep coming back to it whenever I share my story. A theme helps people to walk away from your story remembering ONE main idea. There may be many themes in your story but try to boil it down to just one. Bogging down your soliloquy with multiple main points makes your story muddier, not more poignant.

3. **Clearly present the gospel.** It's a profound tragedy when someone shares their testimony and they don't communicate the gospel in it. This is it! This is your chance to share how someone can come to know God - while they are proactively listening and giving you their attention. Your testimony should communicate to any person listening that God loves them, they are sinful, Jesus is the payment for the penalty of their sin, and they need to trust Christ's payment in order to have a personal relationship with God. That's what happened in your life and it's what can happen in your listener's life. Don't be tempted to leave out this part of your story - it's the most important element. It's the message that changed everything about you and brought you to where you are now, and it's a simple way to explain the finer points of the gospel by telling someone how your life was changed.

4. **Stay away from "Christianese".** (I talk about this in more detail in chapter 18.) *Christianese* is a common term for Christian slang. You know, the words we use all the time in everyday Christian circles that make no sense to others. Terms such as "quiet time," "fellowship," "reconciled" or "walk with God."[34] These terms are confusing to someone who has never heard them and, if we are trying to be clear about what we are communicating, we need to understand the importance of speaking a language that can be easily understood—not leaving people nodding their heads when they really don't have a clue. There is no room for *Christianese* in your testimony.

5. **Have a before, how, and after.** There should be a pretty clear timeline to your story, almost like a plot structure. Talk about what your life was like before Christ, how you met Him,

and what your life is like now. In literary terms, what is the tension? The climax? The resolution? Help your listener by clearly defining how the gospel is woven throughout your story. A timeline is, of course, different for everyone, but it definitely brings a sense of structure to what you're saying, and that helps to keep your listener tracking with you. If you are one of the blessed individuals who came to Christ at an early age, talk about the moment in time when your relationship with God became a daily reality to you, and then point back to the actual decision you made at an early age. This isn't an all-encompassing formula to be followed by everyone, but a timeline will help bring clarity to your story.

6. **Practice, practice, practice!** You should know your testimony by heart without having any note cards or outline in front of you. If someone asks you about your life one day in the shallow end of your public swimming pool, you won't be able to whip out a piece of paper for reference, so have that sucker memorized and be ready to give it at a moment's notice.

Following these guidelines will help to eliminate some of the potential awkwardness you might feel when the time comes to share your story, and it's important to do so.

Don't underestimate the power of your story in another person's life. The story of how God has changed your life can change someone else's life. Isn't that cool? It's really less about "How does the gospel fit into my story?" and more about "How does my story fit into the message of the gospel?" God will use your testimony[35] to affect those around you if you are faithful to speak up.

37
WOMEN AREN'T MEN

Back when I was in college, I discovered something that changed my outlook on life and revolutionized the way that I interacted with people. It was a truth that rested comfortably in front of my eyes for quite some time. And I never really paid much attention to it, until I shockingly and suddenly became enlightened almost all at once. Want to know what that discovery was? Well here it is: men and women are different from one another.

Now, you may think that I'm an idiot because you've known this reality for a long time, but I was truthfully ignorant of it and its stunning ramifications during my formative years in grade school. I plodded along through life as a kid, oblivious to what this fact would eventually mean to me as a man. And I'm really sad to say that I didn't figure it out until I moved into the world of higher education. Knowing it sooner would have probably saved me a lot of embarrassing moments in high school when I presumed that a girl would respond to a given situation in the same way that I would as a dude...always a poor assumption to make, by the way.

But when the scales fell from my eyes and I began to understand for the first time the implications of my discovery, women weren't as scary to me anymore. As I began to explore some of the big differences between the sexes, doorways to wisdom opened up in front of me that had never been there before, leading to less frustration, less confusion, less heartache, and more dates. Yeah, what's up now, suckas?

Let me give you an example of one difference that I discovered. Men are generally good storytellers (not always, but generally) and usually do a great job of inserting appropriate sound effects, advancing and enhancing the story. Whether it's squealing tires on a car or gunfire from a rifle, men just instinctively know how to create good sound effects with their mouth.

Women? Not so much. Have you ever heard a woman try to do sound effects when they're telling a story? It's just awful. And Lord help us all if they try to make a firing gun noise. It usually sounds like a 4 year-old shouting, "Pee-Q!" at the top of their lungs.

Women essentially have two voices in their arsenal. Number one, they have their everyday speaking voice, and number two, every woman has their impersonation of a man voice. Trust me, because I've done some research on this. Every woman has it and it doesn't matter if they're doing an impression of their brother, their dad, their boyfriend, their teacher or their husband. It's always the same across the board and it always sounds like some big, dumb, dopey, drunk gorilla. Seriously, ask any woman to talk like a dude, and you'll get exactly what I just described.

Yes it's true: men and women are different.

Now of course, men have their silly and embarrassing things about them as well, but honestly, there are probably too many to go into and not enough paper to print all of their ridiculous quirks. So in light of that, I will bring us back around again to communicate to you my point: men and women are different from one another. What does that have to do with being in the world and not of the world? I'm glad you asked.

An awareness of this morsel of truth can help you quite a bit in your process of appropriate connection to the world while wisely avoiding emersion in it. An attitude of remaining cautious with the opposite sex when it comes to connecting with them can be easily achieved if you understand that they simply don't think the same as you do. Women process things in a completely different way than men do and vice versa. Of course, this is common sense to most Americans, which is why stand-up comedians will never run out of material. But the fact remains that we are different from one another and embracing this will probably lead you to the conclusion that the best kind of platonic emotional and spiritual connections to be made are those made with the same sex.

Instinctively, I'm better at connecting with men because I am one and I'm not usually trying to show off and be someone I'm not. Honestly, most men do this in the presence of most any woman because of this actuality: we are all idiots.

But being intentional about connecting with members of the same sex makes the most sense because it alleviates the likely awkwardness that springs up in the presence of the opposite gender. A single dude talking to a single girl can create all kinds of weird experiences and signals that are often misread and blown out of proportion on either side. And when a married person is intentional about connecting with a person of the opposite sex, well, that kind of weirdness can be even worse.

I'm not saying that it's written in stone or anything, but a good rule of thumb is to focus on the same sex when trying to connect with people in the world. It sets you up for a lot more clarity in life and a lot less creepy moments brought on by those little things that flood your body called hormones. God calls us to be above reproach in our interactions with the world (Heb. 12:14), so flirting with the line when it comes to the opposite sex can often lead to actual flirting or assumptions of flirting. Why complicate things when we just don't have to?

A reaction to this kind of conservative approach at being in the world but not of it would be the ever-popular eye-roll, common to the indigenous American teenager. *What in the world are you talking about, you loser? You're saying I can't ever talk to a member of the opposite sex that isn't a follower of Christ?*

My retort would be, "Well, you have an uncanny ability to blow things way out of proportion, but no, that's not what I'm saying."

I'm saying that discretion should reign supreme in our efforts to connect with those who need to hear about Jesus. You're probably a smart person, so chances are you know the difference between a casual conversation with someone and a more intimate connection that is made when two people open up to one another. Those kinds of intimate conversations can be extremely dangerous if (a) one party is married or (b) an emotional attachment is made to someone that isn't in the same spiritual realm as you are. Compromising in the area of sexual integrity can only lead to disaster and (by the way) is probably one of the main causes for non-believers thinking we are hypocrites.

If we claim to know Jesus and we say that knowing Him changes us from the inside out, let's live like it and not give temptation any kind of foothold in our lives by inching closer and closer to a line that shouldn't be crossed. Staying away from that line altogether starts with taking the cautious, conservative approach and concentrating our connection efforts in the areas that don't tempt us to compromise our integrity and our witness.

We should aim for nothing less than the kind of witness that magnetically draws people to the Savior. We are the body of Christ, acting as His hands and feet here on the earth and when we strive for upright relationships between the sexes, it's like giving those hands and feet a mani-pedi.

And if you don't understand that last sentence, you're probably an unmarried dude...which proves my point about our differences as men and women all the more.

38
SHOW ME THE FUNNY

Well, I could be wrong, but I believe "diversity" is an old, old wooden ship that was used during the Civil War era.
RON BURGUNDY

Humor is the medium by which people communicate with one another. And I'm not just talking about modern society either. Comedy has been around since humanity was created and will be around into all of eternity. Do I have a bible verse to back up that specific claim? No, but trust me...I've got a very good feeling about this one.

Are you aware that God has a sense of humor? He does. He created humor. Now, I know "funny" isn't a popular thing to attribute to God's creation, but neither is sex and He invented that too. I'm not sure why we shy away from talking about humor in a serious way because it is (and always has been) such an important part of the human experience. Maybe it's because we feel childish when we process funny things in an honest and thoughtful way. There's a constant pressure to "get down to business" and "stop the silliness" when someone wants to be accepted as a mature individual. Heck, even the word *serious* basically means *humorless* when you look it up in the dictionary, and the thought of not being taken seriously makes most people feel disrespected. Thus, humor is usually tossed out the window when talk of a serious God is brought up.

But I think God actually does value humor in a way that we might not expect Him to value it. Why do I presume this to be true? Well personally, I don't need much more proof than the fact that farting is a part of a person's daily routine, but you might need something a little more concrete than I do. Let me give you a few reasons why I believe God appreciates humor.

1. Humor produces laughter, and laughing makes the soul strong.[36] When I think something is funny enough to produce deep belly laughter followed by tears that I wipe from my eyes, I always feel like I'm experiencing life at a deeper level in that moment. The occurrence is rich and almost adventurous. So much so, that I long to duplicate it over and over again just to absorb the kind of life it gives to me. I literally love to laugh, and I'd be willing to bet that you do too. And since laughter is such a large part of strengthening the soul, it is an obvious indicator that the Creator constructed it as a valuable part of life.

2. Humor can be easily found in the bible. There are tons of examples in Scripture that I find funny, but let me highlight four of them for you.

- I Kings 18:27 – This is the quasi-famous Old Testament example when Elijah is mocking the prophets of Baal as they try to get their god to respond by lighting a fire. Elijah basically says, "Maybe he can't hear you right now because he's busy taking a #2...yell louder!" Hilarious, simply hilarious. Elijah may have been the very first stand-up comedian.
- Job 38:21 – Good old-fashioned sarcasm from the mouth of God Himself. God is responding here after Job has questioned where God was in all of his suffering. To paraphrase, the Lord says, "Oh, you know *all* about everything because you were around when the earth was created...right? Oh wait, you weren't!" A verbal backhand to the face of Job probably wasn't pleasant for him, but it sure is funny to the reader.
- 2 Kings 21:23-25 – These verses are so weird that they are

funny. Elisha is walking along, minding his own business when some small boys make fun of the fact that he's bald. Elisha then curses these guys and two she-bears come out of the woods and tear up forty-two of them. The first time I read this, I was like, "What? She-bears?" This story may be bizarre, but you've got to admit that it's funny. Only after I read it again did I commit to never mock a godly bald man with a temper.

- Matthew 7:3-5 – Jesus intentionally uses hyperbole here that undoubtedly produced a snicker or two from the people within an earshot. A log cannot fit into a person's eye and the visual that I get of a huge chunk of wood coming out of someone's face makes me giggle.

3. As I mentioned before, humor is the language that people speak. It is the means by which so many people choose to communicate with one another. If two people are very good friends, they often joke with each other pretty frequently. I know that I do with all of my closest friends. Comedy creates a connection between people and bonds them in a way that nothing else can. God obviously values communication and it's hard to believe that He doesn't really have anything to do with that kind of joyful connection just because it isn't "serious."

4. Humor can break down barriers. Many people know that comedy can be used as a weapon for the wrong purposes, but if it is wielded with godly motivations, it can be a very powerful tool to destroy the walls built up by anger, prejudice, sorrow and hatred. I often employ humor in order to share the gospel with people who have preconceived ideas about what a "religious person" is really like. If someone finds something funny, they will routinely

find the willingness to accept whatever message happens to travel on the heels of that humor. It's an unwritten law of humankind that if you're smart enough to make someone laugh, you're smart enough to have people listen to you. God is very much aware of this fact and I have to believe that He wants us to use humor (with discretion) in order to advance His Kingdom whenever possible.

5. Humor has the ability to disarm sin. When something or someone is laughed at, it is partially robbed of its influence. Think about the school bully getting his pants pulled down in front of everyone in the cafeteria—all of a sudden, he's not so scary anymore, is he? See what I mean? Racism can be stripped of its dominance, idols can be ejected from their thrones, and religion's leverage to sway people toward activity for salvation can be destroyed...all by humor's potential. God values disarming the power of sin and if humor can be used to make that happen, employing it properly is a great thing.

Well, I think I've gone on long enough about the benefits of humor. The bottom line is that it can help you get things done. Comedy is a highly effective tool that is often either underutilized (because of "serious" intentions) or cheapened (by foul language and sexual innuendo). But when taken into the hands of godly men and women who want to shine the gospel into the darkest corners of earth, its power can magnify the beauty of salvation's message.

A friend of mine once said, "Humor has the quality of bringing down walls and defenses so that truth can be clearly communicated." Nailed it.

"Did you hear the one about the..."

IN CONCLUSION...

I'm the kind of person who likes to hang around in the movie theater until the credits are completely done after a film. Most people get up and start making their way to the trash cans and exits as soon as words appear on the screen at the end of a movie, but I feel like you need to get your money's worth, so I stick until the bitter end. (Literally. My feet are usually stuck to the theater floor, covered with Coca-Cola residue.)

Every now and then, toward the end of the credits, there's a fun little extra nugget of film. It's usually only about half a minute long, but it can be relevant to setting up a sequel or just another added joke that the director wants to squeeze in there for the faithful few willing to sacrifice another 5 minutes of their lives watching white text scroll on a black background. It's kinda like the additional french fry you find at the bottom of a fast food bag after you think the meal is all done.

Consider this the extra bit of footage or the single fry at the bottom of the bag.

I'm not an idiot. I realize that the majority of people warming the pews on Sunday morning are not going to proactively make choices to throw themselves into the world and be continuously uncomfortable for the sake of others. On the whole, people just don't work that way...even ones that call themselves fully devoted followers of Jesus Christ.

Consequently, most of the people who will even choose to read a book like this are not going to step outside of their comfort zone and be in the world but not of the world. They will either remain comfortably in their Christian bubble, or become hypnotized by the lure of worldliness and look no different than any other average non-believer.

There are a few, however, who will choose to shake things up. There are always a few. Jesus knew this well…

> *He went on to say, "This is why I told you that no one can come to me unless the Father has enabled them." From this time many of his disciples turned back and no longer followed him. "You do not want to leave too, do you?" Jesus asked the Twelve. Simon Peter answered him, "Lord, to whom shall we go? You have the words of eternal life. We have come to believe and to know that you are the Holy One of God."*
>
> JOHN 6:65-69

In general, when the going gets tough, many will walk away from God. I've seen it many times in my years of ministry, even with the people I thought would never, ever turn their back on Christ.

But there are the faithful few who say to the Lord, "Where else am I gonna go? You and You alone have the words of eternal life. Going anywhere else simply won't be good enough for me."

Perhaps you are one of those few people. Perhaps you will choose to actually do something besides rest in the Christian bubble or melt into the background among the others who don't follow Christ. Perhaps you are like Peter and say, "Lord, to whom shall we go?"

If you are like one of those faithful, do me a personal favor: live as an example of a man or woman who resides in the world but refuses to be conformed to the pattern of the world.

Actually live that out.

Pursue non-believers and pour into their lives. Go all out. And while you do it, be holy as God is holy. It's really the best way to live.

But also recognize that if you do this, many other Christians will *not* be doing the same thing. They will not understand why you choose to spend time with "sinners." They will probably judge you and assume the worst about you in the process of living out your mission. They will subtly ask you to live less radically and slide back into the comfort of being a safe Christian. They will do this because they are scared. Don't be afraid.

Additionally, know that non-believers will, in all likelihood, buck against many of your efforts to connect with them. They will assume that you have some sort of agenda. They will probably have their guard up because they've been burned in the past by overzealous, immature Christians trying to convert them. Keep pressing forward in the face of adversity. Keep loving the hard-to love.

It will be an uphill battle both ways. Believers will question you and non-believers will too. A Christian who is in the world but not of the world has to work hard to do so, but take heart in knowing that the power to live this way comes not from your own effort, but from God the Holy Spirit.

But you will receive power when the Holy Spirit comes on you; and you will be my witnesses in Jerusalem, and in all Judea and Samaria, and to the ends of the earth."
ACTS 1:8A

I am so encouraged when I read verses like this in Scripture. I love knowing that all of this is God's work in the first place and not mine. Jesus continues His mission in us through the mission of the Holy Spirit...my job is to yield to His calling. And when I do, I will know wholeheartedly that my efforts are actually His efforts through me.

The same will be true of you if you say "yes" to living in the world but not of the world. You will likely be awkward in the whole process, but take heart in knowing that God has made you exactly the way He wants you.

I'm awkward. You're awkward. We're all awkward...but that doesn't mean we're incapable of being a key part of God's master plan to redeem the world. I'd rather be awkward and have a front row seat to God's mission than sit in the back row and be boringly comfortable.

You?

SIDE NOTES

[1]One of the 8 definitions that the Bible gives to the word *world* (and that is further described in BDAG) is basically talking about the world lost in sin and that which is hostile to God, wholly at odds with anything divine, and something that is ruined or depraved. It's the actual belief system that one's convictions come from, shaped by sin and in opposition to God. This is what I'm talking about when I say in the *world* but not of the *world*.

[2] Marty McFly, played by Michael J. Fox, in case you were wondering.

[3] This quote comes from a talk I heard Tim Keller give at a conference I was attending with Cru. It might be repeated in one of his many amazing books somewhere, but I heard it when he spoke it live.

[4] As in fickle, volatile, inconsistent, temperamental, or flighty.

[5] This is not the rare opinion of one random woman who teaches in the difficult spiritual environment of the Northeast. It is quickly becoming the predominant spiritual viewpoint of nearly every educational environment in the nation.

[6] Uninteresting, boring, dull, tedious, bland, or lame.

[7] Oswald Chambers, *My Utmost for His Highest.*

[8] Again, this idea came from a talk I heard Tim Keller give at a Cru conference. Needless to say, he shared a lot of amazing thoughts that stuck with me.

[9] By "short phrases," I don't mean jokes mocking the vertically challenged, like my 5'6" self. That would be cruel…even for someone talking in his or her sleep.

[10] I haven't extensively researched this, but I have a hunch that there may have been more than a few students ready to celebrate the termination of the Prohibition era.

[11] I was also responsible for the radio edit of Cee-Lo Green's hit song *Forget You*. (*wink)

[12] More commonly referred to as "The World, the Flesh, and the Devil."

[13] A great continuing metaphor for Jesus as a garbage man, offering to carry out our sin for us, is fleshed out in Peter Kreeft's *Between Heaven and Hell: A Dialog Somewhere Beyond Death with John F. Kennedy, C.S. Lewis & Aldous Huxley*.

[14] The University of Virginia in Charlottesville is notorious for producing extremely intelligent, yet obnoxiously arrogant graduates. The environment on campus at UVA caters to this pompous attitude by calling their freshman, sophomores, juniors, and seniors "first years, second years, third years, and fourth years." Additionally, *campus* is always referred to as *grounds* and *my car* is commonly referred to as *my BMW*. All that being said, the University is a lovely place, and I've known many magnificent people that have attended there…but I'm a Hokie from Virginia Tech, so I have to roast them a little when I get the chance.

[15] That means I'm extremely serious.

[16] My buddy Neil lived next door to Chuck Klosterman in 1991 and claims that his musical nemesis back then was The Eagles. Things change I guess.

[17] The phrase "bless your heart" is defined by Urban Dictionary thusly: A term used by the people of the southern United States (particularly near the Gulf of Mexico) to express to someone that they are an idiot without saying such harsh words.

[18] This is one of the many wise sayings of George Mueller, but I haven't been able to find the specific writing in which it is contained. It is not disputed that Mr. Muller himself said it.

[19] Arnold Toynbee was a British historian, famous for writing a twelve-volume analysis of the rise and fall of civilizations, called *A Study of History, 1934-1961*. A spiritual outlook permeates the *Study* and made it especially popular in the United States for rejecting Greek humanism, the Enlightenment belief in humanity's essential goodness, and the false god of modern nationalism.

[20] Any praise song with "la la la" or "na na na" in it should immediately be stricken from the Sunday morning worship rotation, never to return again. There. I said it.

[21] 1 Corinthians 4:10.

[22] Crawford Loritts (senior pastor at Fellowship Bible Church in Roswell, Georgia) once said, "People who think they can pull themselves up by the bootstraps fail to acknowledge that God gave them the boots *and* the straps." I like that.

[23] This comes primarily by being honest about what your temptations and stumbling blocks are and allowing the Spirit of God to work in and through you to avoid such obstacles. An understanding of the Spirit-Filled life and what it truly means to be a "faith-filled Christian" will change the way you go about your daily journey with God. Many resources can be found on the subject of the Spirit-Filled life, but I recommend *The Wonderful Spirit-Filled Life* by Charles Stanley. Awkward title, awesome book.

[24] Of course, we need to balance this with sensitivity and propriety. See Chapter 16: *If You're Saved and You Know It, Clap Your Hands!*

[25] Although, I often wonder if Jesus would have been a good shortstop.

[26] CruPress.com is a great place to find some of those resources.

[27] Every good and perfect gift is from above, coming down from the Father of heavenly lights, who does not change like shifting shadows. (James 1:17)

[28] According to their website, Chick-Fil-A founder, Truett Cathy, "made the decision to close on Sundays in 1946 when he opened his first restaurant in Hapeville, Georgia. He has often shared that his decision was as much practical as spiritual. He believes that all franchised Chick-Fil-A operators and restaurant employees should have an opportunity to rest, spend time with family and friends, and worship if they choose to do so."

[29] However, the same cannot be said for East-Enders. Think the refined Mary Poppins vs. the Chimney Sweep…Gov-nuh!

[30] What's the difference between England, Great Britain, and the UK? I'm glad you asked. According to About.com, "The United Kingdom is a country that consists of Great Britain and Northern Ireland. In fact, the official name of the country is 'United Kingdom of Great Britain and Northern Ireland.' Great Britain is the name of the island northwest of France and east of Ireland that consists of three somewhat autonomous regions: England, Wales and Scotland. Therefore, England is part of Great Britain, which is part of the United Kingdom. The U.K. includes England, Wales, Scotland, and Northern Ireland. England, Wales, Scotland, and Northern Ireland are not independent countries but the United Kingdom is. The remaining portion of the island of Ireland (that which is not the U.K.'s Northern Ireland) is an independent country called the Republic of Ireland (Eire)."

[31] In this writing, I'm intentionally choosing to ignore any subsequent *Bourne* movies without Matt Damon because they simply don't live up to the original trilogy. Disagree with me if you want to, but in your heart, you know I'm right.

[32] And consequently, I lost a few friends because of my misguided zeal.

[33] John Piper blogs at this web address: http://www.desiringgod.org/blog.

[34] "Testimony" is at the top of the Christianese list.

[35] It's okay for me to use the Christianese word "testimony" here. But don't ever tell a non-Christian, "I'd like to share my testimony with you." They won't get it.

[36] I heard Seattle pastor, Mark Driscoll use that phrase before in a sermon he once gave: "Laughter makes my soul strong", and I couldn't agree more.

ABOUT THE AUTHOR

Shelby Abbott is a Philadelphia based entertainer, public speaker, and author. He is on staff with the ministry of Cru, and his interest in working with college students has led him to speak at campuses all over the United States. Shelby also emcees a variety of conferences throughout the year, blending video, music, and stand up comedy. He has one wife (Rachael), one daughter (Quinn), three houseplants, and a rather impressive LP record collection.

For more information on Shelby, including his blog, log on to shelbyabbott.com.

Check out crupress.com to find Shelby's devotional on sharing the gospel, called *Jacked*.

Made in the USA
Charleston, SC
22 February 2013